THE MEDIUM IS THE MUSE
[Channeling Marshall McLuhan]

Edited by Lance Strate & Adeena Karasick

NeoPoiesis Press, LLC

2775 Harbor Ave SW
Suite D
Seattle, WA 98126-2138

Inquiries:
P.O. Box 38037
Houston, TX 77238-8037

NeoPoiesisPress.com

Copyright © 2014 by NeoPoiesis Press, LLC

All rights reserved. No part of this book may be used or reproduced in any manner whatsoever without express written permission from the publisher except in the case of brief quotations embodied in critical articles and reviews.

The Medium is the Muse: Channeling Marshall McLuhan
ISBN 978-0-9855577-5-1 (pbk)
      978-0-9892018-5-8 (hardcover)
        1. Poetry. 2. Media Studies. I. Strate, Lance. II. Karasick, Adeena.

Library of Congress Control Number: 2014940371

First Edition

Printed in the United States of America.

Cover Design: Milo Duffin and Stephen Roxborough
Interior Layout: Erin Badough and Dale Winslow

Photograph of Marshall McLuhan: Restoration Copyright 2013 Michael McLuhan CPA

Contents

Introduction v

The medium is… 1
    Lance Strate

brush up on yr mcluhan / start dewing it now th medium 8
    bill bissett

Ping-Pong 23
    Tom Wolfe

Man Made Whole Again 24
    Tom Wolfe

All the Information in the Sun 26
    Robert Priest

Short Sound Play 27
    Robert Priest

Micro-Poems 28
    Robert Priest

It Came One Day 33
    Elizabeth McLuhan

Self Reflection 35
    Elizabeth McLuhan

To Sit 36
    Elizabeth McLuhan

Chop Gently 37
    Elizabeth McLuhan

The Purple Rose of Brooklyn Or, Meeting Marshall McLuhan (With a Little Help From Mayan Apocalypse Planet X/Nibiru) 39
    Marleen Barr

McLuhan Kaleidoscope 51
    Mary Ann Allison

Flash in the Pan 56
    John McDaid

Start 58
    Tony Burgess

dear marshall i know you 59
    Stephen Roxborough

Marshalling McLuhan 62
    Lillian Allen

Life 65
    Peter Montgomery

Messy Necessity 66
    Adeena Karasick

In My Blogal Village, Print is Hot 69
    Adeena Karasick

Your Leaky Day 78
    Adeena Karasick

Reader 80
    BW Powe

Technogenie 81
    BW Powe

(lang-gwij)? 86
    William Marshe

Constitution of Silence 88
    Steve Szewczok

we, the real mad poets 89
    Jill McGinn

Late Summer Twilight 91
    Jerry Harp

Pegged to Invisible Consequences............................ 92
    John Oughton

McLuhan's Bride... 93
    David Bateman

The Mechanical Bride's Consolation 95
    Michelle Anderson

Curriculum Vitae.. 98
    Alexandra Oliver

M.F.M.: Media Friend Marshall 100
    Toshio Ushiroguchi-Pigott

I Wouldn't Have Seen It If I Hadn't Believed It: A
Probe Poem... 101
    Andrea Thompson

Dear Mr. Mössbauer, are you online?......................... 106
    Dale Winslow

Silent Resonance 107
    Dale Winslow

It Was Never a Flower to Begin With 109
    Dale Winslow

facebook 110
    Si Philbrook

mY parts.. 111
    John Watts

Prose 112
    Lance Strate

Centenary.. 116
    Lance Strate

Biographies... 119
Acknowledgments... 130

Introduction

As one of the most significant minds of the 20th century, Marshall McLuhan inspired intellectuals, artists, and authors across every imaginable discipline and field of endeavor. While best known for his understanding of media and technology, and the effects they have on the human psyche, sensorium, society and culture, McLuhan's media ecology was grounded in his background as a literary scholar. His inspiration was drawn from the likes of James Joyce, Edgar Allen Poe, Ezra Pound, T.S. Eliot, William Butler Yeats, Wyndham Lewis, Thomas Nashe, and of course William Shakespeare, not to mention the only great work ever produced by committee, the King James Bible. Although he never published any works of fiction or poetry himself, McLuhan was well known for his knack for producing poetic aphorisms and pithy quotations that encapsulate his media poetics, such as

- *Art is anything you can get away with.*
- *The future of the book is the blurb.*
- *Invention is the mother of necessities.*
- *Money is the poor man's credit card.*
- *The new electronic interdependence recreates the world in the image of a global village.*
- *There are no passengers on spaceship earth. We are all crew.*
- *We look at the present through a rear-view mirror. We march backwards into the future.*

And of course,

- *The medium is the message.*

Celebrated in his own time as the media guru, oracle of the electronic age, and Canada's intellectual comet, it is not surprising that celebrations were held all around the world over the course of the year 2011, marking the 100th anniversary of McLuhan's birth. And the biggest celebration of all was held in the city that McLuhan called home for most of his career, Toronto. Organized by Dominique Scheffel-Dunand, Director of the University of Toronto's McLuhan Program in Culture and Technology, the McLuhan Centenary Conference and DEW Line Festival included an evening of performance poetry curated by Andrea Thompson, and featuring bill bissett, David Bateman, Lillian Allen, Alexandra Oliver, and Adeena Karasick, co-editor of this collection, with yours truly as Master of Ceremonies. That event provided the nucleus and the impetus to edit an anthology of writings both creative and cerebral inspired by Marshall McLuhan. And building on that nucleus, we gathered together original work and some previously published pieces from the McLuhan community and the media ecology network, along with a bit of the cartoon art that McLuhan hailed as an exemplary form of cool media. And what better press to put this volume out than NeoPoiesis, whose motto, *celebrating the independent, creative mind*, is so very consonant and resonant with McLuhan's method, his probes and percepts, and his distinctive mode of expression.

    McLuhan was fond of the Ezra Pound quote, *the artist is the antenna of the race*, and with this in mind, seized upon the metaphor of the Distant Early Warning Line, a set of radar stations set up by the United States in Canada, Alaska, Greenland, and Iceland during the Cold War to detect incoming bombers and missiles that might cross the Arctic from the Soviet Union. He published the *Marshall McLuhan DEW-Line Newsletter* from 1968 to 1970, providing his insights about current events and advice on critical thinking and creative problem solving; a Distant Early Warning card deck intended as an aid in decision-making was produced during this period as well. And McLuhan long maintained that artists, visual, musical, and literary, were the best sources of insight into understanding media, and the total media environment, and that arts education was the best way to train individuals to deal with the blasts and counterblasts generated by the maelstrom of contemporary culture and technology. The arts, he argued, could constitute an anti-environment that can stand in sharp contrast to the ordinary world that we typically take for granted. Our everyday environments, being part of our normal routines, easily fade into the background and fall outside of our awareness, becoming functionally invisible to us. Creative expression and exploration have the potential to rouse us from our somnambulistic state, waking and shaking us up, making us pay attention to what is going on all around us. And this is especially needed in light of the constant barrage of information and entertainment, and even more so the endless onslaught of innovation and change that we have been and continue to be subjected to.

With this vital understanding in mind, we have gathered together a group of poets, writers, and artists who understand that *the medium is the muse*, which is to say that the medium is a source of inspiration, and who in one way or another are *channeling Marshall McLuhan*, who regard McLuhan as both medium and muse. And it is our sincere hope that this collection that you hold in your hands will divert and delight, provoke and incite, stir and stimulate, arouse and instigate, and above all inspire you to further thought and exploration, and especially to acts of creative imagination.

Lance Strate, 2013

Lance Strate

The medium is...

The medium is the message
McLuhan's wake-up call
warning us to be aware
of the way that we get things done
because the way that we do things
determines what we end up doing
and the way that we do things
determines what we end up with
when we do the things that we do

The medium is the massage
McLuhan's pun and word play
our technologies work us over
manipulating our senses
remixing sensibilities
we shape our tools
and our tools shape us
individually and collectively

The massage splits into the mass age
from the Gutenberg galaxy
comes the age of the machine
the age of the masses and the massive
where the individual is an isolated
alienated atom
within the nuclear family
a corporate conformist
lost in the midst of a lonely crowd

And message divides into mess age
and we have made a massive mess of things
the global village a global garbage dump
McLuhan called it *Planet Polluto*

Lance Strate

Except now
Pluto is no longer a planet
and soon enough
the same may be true of planet Earth

The maelstrom
McLuhan's metaphor
for our technological and cultural environment
a whirlpool of
advertising
entertainment
information
and news
but there are patterns recognizable
within the dynamic mess
although immersed within the chaos
still we can find emerging order
provided we pay attention

Alfred Korzybski said
the map is not the territory
media are maps
they tell us about territories both real and imagined
different media map the world in different ways
each one shaping our view of the world differently
altering our sense of place
and space
orienting
disorienting
directing
and misdirecting

Neil Postman said
the medium is the metaphor
and
our metaphors create the content of our culture
and so

we come to see ourselves
our minds and our bodies
as writing tablets
or clockworks
or steam engines
or electric circuits
or as computers

Ashley Montagu said
in teaching
it is the method
and not the content that is the message
the drawing out
not the pumping in
he understood that the questions we ask
give us the answers that we get
or as the computer scientists say
garbage in, garbage out

New modes of communication
result in new forms of social mutation
writing erases the tribal world
inscribes us into civilized, city life
printing produces the modern world
nationalism and industrialism
and the electric circuit
binds us together as global villagers
and actors on a global stage

New media result in
an ongoing metamorphosis
Walter Ong says
human consciousness evolves
we are transformed
from tradition-directed orality
to inner-directed literacy
to the plugged in

participating
outer-directed
people of the tube and the web

Show me the money and I'll show you the medium
the first coins followed the alphabet
paper money is a product of the printing press
and with computers and telecommunications
all that is solid
about cash and capital
melts into the air
and is gone.

One evening after a seminar with Neil Postman
I went out to a bar with my classmates
went to the Men's Room,
and saw graffiti on the wall that said:
pornography is technology's contribution to masturbation
and I said
the ghost of Marshall McLuhan was here!

Online and the on the air we go meatless
in person, our bodies are our media
as are our organs of perception
the ear thrusts us into the midst of things
at the center of action
surrounded by acoustic space
while the eye places us on the outside looking in
as spectators, voyeurs, and peeping Thomists

Media are tools for thought
every language contains its own unique worldview
written language brings linearity and abstract thinking
words, numbers, pictures, music
all encode the world in different ways
Isadora Duncan said

Lance Strate

*If I could tell you what it meant
there would be no point in dancing it*

Oral cultures remember collectively
through songs and poetry
stories and sayings
the written record gives us
chronology and history
and now, memory is a database
randomly accessible
hyper and nonlinear
easily erased
and yet capable of recording
anything and everything
any of us say or do

Our media come from us
they are extensions of us
they are reflections of us
but we forget
we think our technologies are alien
apart from us
we fall in love with them
not knowing that we have fallen in love with
an image of ourselves
McLuhan called this
Narcissus narcosis

Through our media
we learn what the meaning of *is* is
formal cause: the pattern that directs
when every effect is special.
the calendar and the clock
the written word
the printed page
telescope
microscope

and the electromagnetic wave
all tell us
all about
space and time

Our media are extensions of ourselves
they come between ourselves and the world
they screen and filter the world
Max Frisch said
*technology is the art
of never having to experience the world*
but what comes between ourselves and our world
becomes our world
and so we become what we behold
because the medium is the membrane

The medium divides
the medium connects
the medium comes in between
in the gaps and the intervals
in the ground behind the figure
the medium surrounds and pervades
the medium is the environment
we enter *into* a conversation
we write *in* English or Spanish or French
we *get into* a book or movie
we *go* online
and we study media *ecology*

The medium is Marshall McLuhan
the medium is he
as the medium is you
as the medium is me
and the medium is all of us together.
so let's be the medium
and spread the message

It's a Rare Medium, Arthur Asa Berger

bill bissett

bill bissett   brush up on
     yr   a long
             pome
mcluhan
   pomebig
         type

th medium is th
    message
  start dewin it   now
    i like mine
   reelee well dun
     how abt yu

is that medium rare

bill bissett

brush up on yr mcluhan / start
dewing it now   th medium

is th message a long pome big type
  is that medium rare   or well dun
   eye like it veree well dun how abt yu

   mess with th sage turn it 2 medium n
   median yes uv th hot cathode ray tubes
   what hes saying th teknolojee is th nu
    latest or bcumming redundant behaviour
soshul n individual   oh we wer huntrs n
gathrers thats how we wer thn th agrikultural
revolushun n th industrial r evolushun th
invensyun uv steem yu give me steem heet
  n childrn sew great getting in2 thos hard 2
  get at spaces in th coal mines evreewun gets
  teebee thn we eez in2 th evreewun gets teevee
pre during n now post compewtr revolushyuns
we have th xpertise now 2 distribute food
evreewher dew we yet have th politikul will
  all th isms battling it   out   all th adaptiv n
  mal adaptiv inkreesinglee evn latherd with
nostalgias bcum de trop thr is wun familee
farm left n its ekonomiklee   creatid soshul
 n familial binaree posessif   lingrs as dew all
th isms preskripsyuns slingr   pointlesslee in us
   like th appendix yet may   make us act in out
uv date wayze what   wev   past we oftn will go

   back 2 as we keep on changing mores nu n
old patterns sequens each rev creates nu
   mores n soshul behavious patterns n behav
i
our

bill bissett

   mcluhan thee pioneer on how teknolojee
changes us n we bcum th cathode ray tubes
  soothe bathe yr brain bcum th telephone
n being as he prediktid prfekt 4 indoktrin
   ating what they usd 2 call brainwashing
ths brain   needs 2 b klensd uv previous

  teknolojeez soshul politikul templates
is n was n th nu us   get with th nu
  thing th latest tekno   identitee change
up brain washing sew   great thank god
 we have masheens 4 ths now brain wash
 ing isint veree hard 2 dew politikul
  ordring crowd control uv othrs who
 have less keep them down memoree stik
post modernism contains all thees memor
 eez tropes admonishyuns n mor n brand
 nu things we carree them all th teknolojee
  is us whats next mor as it cums in2 us

 mcluhan was in the line up 4 th great moovee
  annee hall also th great moovee videodrome
   wher peopul shove videos in theyr bellees
    didint he predikt th closing uv all block
bustr stores soon peopul will have no need
  2 leev theyr houses n just as well as its
sew pollutid out ther   espeshulee if netflix
   content improovs n   evreething can b
downloadid yes wev bin   a long time out
uv th vizual age longr sins   th literate epoch
 its not onlee aquarian its   post agrarian
evreething was langwage   thn n langwage
  was evreething thn yu ar   my evreething
courtlee love stabil work ford fors mono
 gomee
    antiquarian   thn all th evreething was

bill bissett

   mor pickshur less talk   thn pixils th med
ium is th message no longr   faktoreez ordrs
    faktoree mill mine towns jobs 4 life poor
row houses smoke stacks   dirtee air watr
   4sure th medium can b soothing th rays
themselvs resepsyun alwayze welcum in
   ths is what we all look at ths is what we all
heer takes care uv us dew it ths way n
     yul b fine   kool medium   consuming
without fuming n can lack kritikul fakultee
lacking kritikul fakultee is veree helpful 2
   th elite peopul n sheep can follo ordrs
reelee well th medium is n duz bring th
    message s

sew th inkreesing need 4 media literasee
th lmedium is th teknolojee n is th orakul we
love on th evolushyunaree thrust greed is
 nevr gud is nostalgia 4 accumulaysyuns uv
precious   previous   paranoia templates
eras
 is ar out
 ovr soon   out uv date now
dusint help evreething is a try out try in
  mcluhan med i um mu i i um dem mi u
dem mu med ed mmi mu why was th bride
   sew mechanikul madonna in toronto on th
red carpet told tiff volunteers 2 not look at
   her 2 avert theyr gayze onlee a vowel
change mcluhan mclohan lindsey whn th
   condishyuns change th identitee changes
wuns eye was in first yeer sayanz th medium
   guidid us thru lovlee 4est place path we wer
on we all sew n herd th voice uv a prson
   who had gone thru n oh it was sew beautiful
ther she sd n sew hard 2 accept at first 2

bill bissett

   go thru oh wer not alive aneemor nooo
with th advent uv th printing press standard
   izd spelling bcame important 4 setting up
th keys each lettr had its own key set lettrs 4
   a passing comet n pixils fragments our
latest metaphor 4 ourselvs   ohhh
   now watching th gop debates th vizual
respons is that a rug that leedr is weering
   n is his seconds at a time onlee xpressyun
can he hold that longr wasint th groom
      mechanical as well
texting changes korrektness
   spelling n

evreething meening   jumps see it go up
th disapeering s all   bottom n top middul
   individualism dissolving in2 tribalisms whn
tribalisms what   ar tribalisms dissol
ving is th global village reelee opn 4
   bizness is ths th
last dance is ther way mor play all th typog
   rapheez all th back wards n 4wards trending

now
all th possibul retro ideaz refitting retooling
what n with from kleeshay 2 arketype n back
 agen ths partikular idea on a slant or bias
cud look great
with ths unusual idea 4
   soshul class   harmonee as radikul as it mite
b 4 late   evning   weer cud bloom in
   spring side   bar is love proprietal or
proprietee th   eparrish or village proprtee pro
pensitee t   h prior n th proprietree is
   she he a   gud an owning replika uv linking

bill bissett

consistent sex   with proprtee a kiss
2 build a reems   n   reems uv papr play or
edocumentz whn   duz a kiss bcum a
   kontrakt a disapeer   ing tree if its sew much
grooming n brindel bridel   love turtul dove can
     it evr b proprietee or sum
        proprietal ium just asking how mono
    ismono go mee n what is love sew manee
   approaches is it part   uv th message s is th
kontrakt th teknolojee   from klee shay 2
arke type n back agen as we ar all deeplee trying
    2 get our lives in th global theatre
    how we change with th teknolojee

n   with th changing trajektoreez uv our
    ekonomik soshuling agreed upon n dis
agreed on models uv produktivitee n dis
    tribusyuns with th   changing revolushyuns
gathring n hunting   agrikultural industrial
     literate vizual   elektronik compewtr post
   compewtr evree wun out uv th hous
evreewun working 4 less n less working
    all th gendr roles hypotheseez change
as th ekonomik soshul trajektoreez uv
    post modernism evreething in th mix
n th perjorativ price uv proprietree dont take
  it

prsonalee petunia parsimonious n parker pend
rickul passengrs obsessyun possessyun oh th

    proquinitee uv it all n th qwestyun lingrs if its
proprietee or tree is it love   can it b a th answr
     is b tho cud it b a meer   bagatel askd l
    th changing teknolojeez   all th wepons
  improoving ovr time evn is   th media how we

13

bill bissett

       massage it th media relentlesslee n change
with th teknolojee changing changing us
    espeshulee as th arketype is a kleeshay
is an internalizaysyun uv a specifik
    ekonomik hierarkikul ordring th
      parametriks uv n th guidans
        change with th change did we
 get enuff change uv teknolojee
will we bcum calmr n mor sereen n benign
 with serenitee deepning n view all tek
    nolojeez media as
themselvs points uv view can we catch
  th tailoring up with our own brains
culturalee creatid
    selvs tetrads wikipedia entr
what duz th media retreev that had bin
   obsolescent erleer what duz th media flip
in2 whn on th bout bias
pushd 2 xtreems turn on tune in n drop
  out or in marshall mcluhan sd that first b4

                            t leary
sew brush up on yr mcluhan start dewin it
 in th changing now th class war is th theatr
    how
is th seething arrangd th uppr crust uv th pie
  has boxes if we can put them in th back th
  mddul n poor can go in th   front evreewun
gets 2 what it is 2 b sum wun els see how
  they go who is we tho   mcluhan knew
teevee was   a sedativ if that b xcellent also
 a dangr 2 kritikul thinking th Gutenberg
   galaxee   undrstanding media b kool
reel kool west side storee whn yr a jet or

a capulet th dangrs uv tribalism sum
   uv thees chairs make me shortr

bill bissett

  sum make me tallr in ords othr words
    wods wots just as sum kleeshays can n
  may bcum arketypes th arketypes typo
    grapheez types lettrs 2 an arriving
  comet may bcum kleeshays was
    jung reelee jungr thn springtime
      chins ovr th taybul worlds

    if pariah needbee
obviouslee thn we change with n in
korporate internalize changes with th
changing teknolojeez what wer yu
dewing in th agrikultural revolushyun
now its genomes that can save us n we
ar not on th farm wch whn it was sew
  happning farm life diktatid shaped
our soshul mores arrangements n we
now farm out mores   as it cums in
our arketypes n kleeshays shay pas
    ma sd test me tubular

  th geneticist is in

ar we heer by design or is it a close cut
n farmr brown will let us have th barn
  In our minds wher evreething happns
illustraysyuns   th nucleosis uv th
  monogram pickshur ths
  uv th mechanikul bride n groom
  what theyv memorizd 2 resite

1 peopul famileez standing in circuls
      listning
2 each othr singing round th piano
      sheet mewsik
2 peopul famileez sitting in circuls
l   istning 2 th radio

bill bissett

3 peopul famileez watching teevee ma
n pa watching ovr evreewun watching
4 fathrs mothrs know best th last ord as
   brout down from th kastul th nuspapr
th mansyun th elite th citadel th state th
   god manuskript religyun hand me
        down
   th wording ord word th rod w sparring
 th digital rev digitalis
   evreething is cumming trew
we carree all thees templates from previous
adaptaysyuns   out uv date with us heart
breking that can b replacements 4 n we take
a deep breth n go on   adaptiv n mal adaptiv
   still hunting n gathring n yet not reelee
primal n   yet not n we save evreething
   carreeing it all
4ward sew poignant our wastes destroying us
 n th othr animals still mc teknolojeez that may
not hurt sew much still loyal like manee
republicans n conservativ bow 2 out uv date
 consepts like bizness first in all cases th market
is nevr wrong song
we sift thru thees having children will keep us
 2gethr loving them will not hurt

   nothing will hurt if we dew it rite what is rite
each day now is reelee a nu day can we find
   share n
 moov on is
romantic love mor mechanikalee proprietal mor
   thn we thot
bingul bangul or periferal wch
as we oftn still go dysfunksyunal
with its suddn wrench n deep disapointments
   can we rise above let go seek th nu teknolojee

bill bissett

we cant evn yet predikt uv our klinging
   neurolojeez
     will it b no reptilian fold
       will it b th gold in our spirits
    who can say what it will b
  romantik love or less mor
who dusint want it aneewa
  n evn if its a realm we pass
thru alm n alma realther is no answr
     despair
ther is no answr   joyousness   ther is no answr
why wundr isint it worth it what is worth empiricists
dont like dea x masheena spiritualists can n dew
   if yu want 2 change
 yr life yu change yr life she sd 2
me   keep on ther is no answr jokes laffs
   serious gaffs

profound heart breks if yu dew ths
   aktivitee that
result will happn reelee that as in serious
disastr   a serious gap an eezee bite not
2 b reducktiv
skulls n serious disolushyun
     regardless

dere princess rosa yes fr sure if love is not
  proprietaree or parrish priorlee a priori
   proprietal   n thats not reelee love but e
documentaysyun sex as ownrship   leeding 2
proprtee can we own another prson   if its love
 can it b proprietal or th appropriate   appropriay
syun uv anothr prson can it b appropri ate priapus
ate priape th proprtee or th proprtree uv   th love
 as not proprtee proprlee th proprietor   proprie
tree th proprtee or th proprtree uv th love as not

17

bill bissett

proprtee not proprlee th proprtee uv th proprie
  taree proprietal yet we ar alwayze entrtaining n
sew I magining reel love as not propetree t fees
    4 proprietree proprietree yes whn th ekonomik
bases 4 proprietal propr treed love dissolv thn
  that will as hunting n gathring has in   manee
places following by   agrikultural revolushyun
   supplantid by th   Industrial n th elektronik n th
compewtr skreen   cyber space n th post com
  pewtrs inkreesing   alredee eye diseeses th
literate acompaneeing th courtlee   love n
  proprtee th industrial childrn sew greatin th
       mines they cud get in2 all thos
small spaces n ther was no wun like them
4 chimnee sweeping   n th peopul dying uv
  teebee n thn th compewtr n post   vizual post
compewtr revs   evreewun out   uv th hous
evreewun needs 2   work 2 pay   th bills
  evreewun back   in2 th hous evreewun
       evn   hauntid by th past hunting
needs 2 work at home   its   sew cheepr 4 th
   bosses   all th gendr roles changing   as th

needs uv th work fors benefits ar yu kidding me 4

  th elite th tops changing now what le next is
proprietal   approp riaysyun   uv proprietee a
 priori parish   proprietal n proprietree echo
subsequent 2 th plentiful n   oftn prsonal prsona
liquiditee sew priaptik yes   see all th evn virtual
propinquitee was eveething   well n proprlee treed
sew manee wer asking th qwestyun reel love is
  kontextual   n without kontext yes greetree free
     uv text texting
         exiting what can we dew
     know owning love gud gus chattul bettr best th

bill bissett

    dark is bed sighd gud wife uv gus look 4 th pome
     in th meteor drawr n th   sacrifice comment wher
is th opning avenu or exit   top seekr th adventur
     is in th maintenens   who sz mechanikul bride
n sew grooming a s well   nostalgia   n ar thees
  qwestyuns onlee within langwage n that alwayze
       changing n what we   think we know
 abt his her storee sirtinlee   changing teknolojeez
    create   n ar creating n changing ideas
   re
what is permanent n shifting sifting thru models
  uv be havyur test testing tubular what needs
uv what falling away sway   dissolving th sounds
  uv comfort in th magnesium   coastal bye
products
     n pro
  tekting th safetee uv who we ar with what march
ideas models behave   from farming in 2 framing
     out skreens skreens evreewher screens
      all evree   wher its a skreen we ar in
front uv filing fillng what remnants n fragments
   dee teriarating cyber spaceyusness thers a
    clustr uv eez strangelee reepeeting n heeding
      in2 a black hole   th need 2 love wher
   2 take that n th 2 share proprtee will not
        alwayze follow
   in fakt fallow may have alredee started
       2 fall away sew
propadilinquent ganda filling sumptuous display
  us
mouthing anakronism aftr anakronism as th
  ekonomik

   n soshul template ordrs ordrings uv th politikul
     soshul relaysyun 2 proprietal produktivitee

bill bissett

paradism paradigm   model style as papagano
papagana our arms around flautist fleet n sleek
  sleet as ths gorz ths nu wun bettr   ar alwayze
changing getting sopplantid su planting
      i like 2 think love   s not proprietal
    proprietree freez   prop propellar poprertree
  but ium seeing in othrs in   recent yeers thats a
      large parts parse   uv what it is
n th kodependenseez   sure is that a nostalgia
or   what it is peopuls behavyurs 4 sure i love
    parsing   in th n a nu retro refitting reclaiming
   n paws in th   last danse is ths th last danse i
          askd th taxi drivr n   he sd
  yes thers maybe 50–60 yeers left 4 our speces
    will we blow each othr up eye askd no he sd
      probablee from pollushyun sew dew
          we enjoy each day say
        each nite as we can   no nu danse
    beginning i like   2 think love is reelee   sharing is
mor proprlee reprsuasivlee n reelee not owning
        anothr prson is
sharing without punishing howevr i cant proov that
  its what i like 2 think hmmm funnee yu ask abt ths
    i was have bin asking ths myself   uv kours ther
  ar sew manee kinds uv   love frend love god love
romantik love   child love adult love sex love teechr
love student love
      boss love koleeg love n all uv   thees loves
changing countree love wuns countree love world
        love yes helping   love   being helpd love
        living love dying love changing love self
    love sew
much torments sew much joyousness living love
all thees loves changing how manee times have
  i told yu she he asking how manee times what
s th deel is it onlee wretchid kodependenseez not

bill bissett

      enuff self work n that lack leeking in2
      disturbans
worth wo no its not reelee reducktiv its th thrill uv
      submersyun n all ths huge time alone n n n
 soon

uh uh uh uh uh th skreens gone whatevr will we
 dew   oh lookit all th skreens went out whatul we
   dew th awakening or th switch off 2 sumthing
harshr or is softr mor   wide eyed wundr mor silkee
  soothing she sighd n   mr swetr sd 2 him i wud
reelee like 2 get in2   sumthing mor comfortabul
with yu   evn thn merging   i think all we can dew
is 2 stay in tuned tuning   less aware uv th arabella
  dichotomeez rangr get   with it put our bettr best
foot 4ward
 as they used 2 say n carree on
   arabesque dulcimer meditating
reed how th parrots rise 2 such   palpitating
   murmurs
ther sunrise aftr sunset n th perlee dawn wings ovr
 raptyur sing xercise whatevr all th things n mor we
can dew tai chi swimming working counselling being
counselld nowun heer is who yu think they ar or   yu
wanting them 2 b they ar who they ar awesum   tru
      buld strangelee self interestid n
          justifying n want in wanting n
   letting go n chilling its all sew how it is
  love them that wayze we cant make them
   xtensyuns uv us theyr not an xtensyun uv us i
am lookin at yu   yu ar not me yr lookin at me ium not
   yu   who ar yu
wer just lookin at each   othr hello whats yr name
n what dew eye know less   thn nothing thanks sew
much 4 all thos brilliant   times in van hope yu ar
   raging n xcellent thanks 4 sharing thos xcellent

bill bissett

    adventurs by th pacifik as we go on qwestyuning
th media n th message s n th messengr s lots uv
love n thanks mr bill   teknolojee is love princess
   rosa   sighd

ps is love proprietal or is that loves proprietee n is
a priori from th last bunga low on th left leeving th
   parrish is wher is th prior itee delishus dish thot
priapus priapay in th prioree not love reelee thn
   what is love sharing oh th propinquitee n th cal
umnee shouldrs shovuls n with out owning reelee
or poss essif letting go n letting b n letting n being
with th at wun prson n without claiming as hard

as it sum times is can b it can n that love dusint
   have bene fits is alredee benefitting   sheesh
   xcellent media
               attensyun span 3 seconds
   most prsuasiv propaganda best adds wins
  eleksyun   no time 4 kritikul fakultee did yu see
th moovee th   fakultee with piper laurie it was
  great   sew trew 2 life
whatevr oh th skreens went out whatevr will we
    dew all th skreens went out or th switch
  went   out is it 2 sumthing softr or harshr oh eye
dont know or th switch   went off 2 sumthing
els is it harshr or softr   oh i dont know i dont
know n   no binaree th awakening awakening
ium sew prsuadid o th switch went off 2 sumthing
    els mor thn proprlee   propelling o i dont know
      oh
   i dont know dilecksyuns trilecksyuns i dont
    know
      as befits th tremulaysyuns n
        th aegis uv marchallows

Tom Wolfe

Ping-Pong

I walked into the living room.
They rocked me with a stereo boom.
No haven here downstairs at all.
Nymphets frug on my wall-to-wall
And boogaloo in my private den
And won't let poor work-a-daddy-in.

How glorious!
Übermenschen! golden gulls!
With transistor radios plugged in their skulls.
Radiant! with an Elysian hue
From the tubercular blue of the television.
Such a pure Zulu euphoria
Suffuses their hi-fi sensoria!

How glorious.
I shall stand it long as I can,
This neo-tribal festival.
Their multi-media cut-up,
The audio-pervasion of their voices,
Leaves me with two choices:
Shall I simply make them shut up—
Or . . . extrapolate herefrom the destiny
Of Western Man?

Tom Wolfe

Man Made Whole Again

I gazed upon the printed page.
It tore me limb from limb.
I found my ears in Mason jars,
My feet in brougham motorcars,
My khaki claws in woggy wars—
But in this cockeyed eyeball age
I could not find my soul again.
Vile me,
And then—
           I touched a TV dial
And—pop!—
           it made me whole again.

tvman, Dean Motter

Robert Priest

All the Information in the Sun

All the information in the sun
Cannot disappear forever

From the universe
Deny light all you like

The dark data shows up anyway
Under your lids

Under your feet
In the part of your palm

You can't read
You can't know enough

Dark data to predict
Its effect on any future

Matter
The road may or may not be there

At the next step
The journey may go on

Whether or not you disappear
Into the distance

Robert Priest

Short Sound Play

Unheard over the multiple very loud soundtracks all playing at once through various sound systems two people in silhouette gesticulate urgently, trying to talk to one another. Stage is dark except for whatever lights there are in various appliances and media systems. Eventually one of the people goes over to the stereo system and turns it off. Now loudest among the many remaining sounds is the blaring and distorted announcing coming from the TV. The other person turns that off too. The shriek of a smoke alarm now rises to the fore. Then it is a blender in the kitchen that has been left on perhaps with crystals in it. Now that it's turned off we can hear the sound of the air conditioner clanking. Then it is the sound of a fan. When this is turned off we hear a baby crying. The mother runs from the room and suckles the baby so that the baby stops crying. When the baby stops crying we hear a chorus of crickets chirping outside. An owl is hooting. The sounds grow louder and louder. Suddenly the crickets stop. We begin to discern a faint whistling sound. The owl stops. The whistling increases in volume. The man closes the window. The sound has become shrill and ominous. It grows louder and louder until it is all we hear. The people with the baby are huddling under a table. There is a huge flash of light and then flickering light, as of flames. Ten people are screaming in agony at once some as though nearby, others as though in adjacent houses. One person stops. Now the loudest voice is someone begging and whimpering. When that person stops we discern the cries of another and another until at the very end we hear the wailing of the baby. The crying of the baby gets louder and louder until it splits open and becomes two babies and the two babies become four as the multitude exponentially increases not only in number and volume but in its capacity to express pain and terror.

Robert Priest

Micro-Poems

Brevity forever
·
Fragm
·
cellf
·
Disarmageddon
·
Eupheminism
·
Faith sex
·
D(rugged) individualism
·
Viral or spiral?
·
For sale: previously feared darkness
·
Trying to get Jesus to walk on water in a laboratory
·
You can't point everywhere at once
·
With the increasing information has come an equal increase in inattention
·
A loincloth is a kind of space suit
·
When people tell you they are gullible do you always believe them?
·
Next year in dystopia
·

Robert Priest

Wishing wellness

·

The first thing god wants from us is a beginning

·

Every herd has its cliff

·

What doesn't kill me just delays the inevitable

·

Wickedness loves stupidity

·

One end of the rope blames the other for the knot

·

No two people see the same miracle

·

Everything takes forever

·

If humankind were kind

·

I can see into the present

·

I believe in life before death

·

The ever prescient moment

·

I'm so far out I have to pull the envelope

·

Give it while you can

·

It is better to have loved and loved and loved

·

I like the "ask you" in m-ascu-line

·

I like the "in in" in feminine
Never in human history have so many people been in life with one another

·

Robert Priest

Our secret power is our compassion
.
Empathy equals
.
It is all one vast serendipity
.
Maybe you should start listening to your outer child
.
Look big and carry a little Taser
.
Would you like a little assault with that pepper spray?
.
The bomb that only destroys poetry is called poetry
.
The only true poetry is in the longing for poetry
.
Avant-garde is the new orthodoxy
.
The emperor's new poems
.
Every other day god and the devil switch jobs
.
It is the curse of the capable — not to be called upon
.
Is easier to crush hope than to have it
.
I'm not sure if I want certainty or not
.
The elephant in the room is the monkey on my back
I don't need anyone to help me celebrate
interdependence day
.
In my country we don't have free speech but the
speech we do have is really really cheap
.
Whispering is not just a right it's a duty

Robert Priest

- Everything before the written word was pre-text
- If DNA had spell-check there'd be no evolution
- There is absolutely no slave labour in the making of these chains
- I choose free will
- Turn the other other cheek
- Please do no stare at the observers
- The poor inherit the rich
- If it wasn't for stumbling I would hardly walk at all
- I'm practising obstinence
- If you can't take love you can't make love
- Sisyphus makes everything a hill
- Some call it reincarnation — some call it recidivism
- This dream is unavailable at the present time, please try again later
- I see the gun as completely empty... for good... forever
- Hell is better if you're cheerful
- The reason time/space is curved is because it's made of smiles

Robert Priest

- Backwards Sisyphus is still Sisyphus

- With a star on my stick and a breakaway on an open sky

- The body and the brain are mutual maps and there is no territory

- The sky is a search engine with only one name in it: the beloved

Elizabeth McLuhan

It Came One Day

     it came one day
exploded in my head
a silent Hiroshima
mushroom form dissolving
and dispersing throughout
my entire atmosphere
my body's nations
and my nervous networks
splintered and disrupted
connections all cut dead

does it matter who finally pushed the button?

my aching leg
the dizzy spell
the crazy cracking headache
no matter now
I am done
the little atom bomb
inside me
had no alternate escape
I'd stored it and ignored it
far too long
--
it's had its day in infancy
now my blood glistens
with its poison
bones ring
with its fatal song

and how I pull myself together
picking up the rubble and debris

Elizabeth McLuhan

carefully arranging it
like some old whore
primping before a mirror
—me—the mistress of my madness
and how the marquis grins
how my little histories
(beloved bastards)
grow hysterical
are screaming from the pain
radiation burned and scarred almost beyond recognition
they limp and crawl within my brain

such a catastrophe
and no one know it's happened
except me—and
—to all appearances
I was only home alone
again watching tv

Elizabeth McLuhan

Self Reflection

self reflection
flattens out your face
reduces all your
curves to lines
that cannot
be erased

your mirror
is a magic box
transforming
all your fright
your image has
a hundred locks

you suffocate
at night

Elizabeth McLuhan

To Sit

to sit
and talk
of things
and of events
delays of events
delays the moment
that must finally come
the awkward emptiness
the silent present tense

full ripe
with revelation
of reality and sense

how fingers hum
and skins communicate
their scents
and thoughts
float free
in pools
within the eyes

and words
so wasted once
and dense

lie quiet now
and as they die
repent

Elizabeth McLuhan

Chop Gently

chop gently as you kill
for think of all the blood that you might spill
upon your spotless hands
chop gently

kill extra if you must but not too few
your customers are pleased with what you do
and they all want their policies renewed
kill extra

starve quiet when not fed
for the faintest cry of pain might wake the dead
or stir the living
starve quiet

no matter what you see be silent
it's not life but only news that's really violent
or so the hangman said
be silent

Mars, Dean Motter

Marleen Barr

The Purple Rose of Brooklyn Or, Meeting Marshall McLuhan (With a Little Help From Mayan Apocalypse Planet X/Nibiru)

"We live science fiction"—*Marshall McLuhan*

      I think it all started when my mother described how much she enjoyed chatting with Eleanor Roosevelt while shopping in Arnold Constable. Her narrative about sitting directly behind the Duke and Duchess of Windsor on the opening night of *Oklahoma* also piqued my interest. My mother, secure in the knowledge that she was a Jewish American Empress incarnate, had the supreme *chutzpah* to demand that the Duchess remove her over the top stage view blocking hat. Such is the origin of my love for interacting with famous personages and contemplating how people's paths cross.

      I had to wait until I was a graduate student in English at the University of Michigan before I could tell a celebrity interaction story which equaled the ones my mother told me. After hearing that Jorge Luis Borges was going to speak at Michigan State University, I high tailed it due north to Ypsilanti. I sat in the MSU theater and gasped when I saw an elderly rotund figure with cane in hand enter stage left. I was seeing *Borges*. I couldn't believe it. As soon as his lecture ended, I searched for a telephone to apprise my mother about my Borgesian experience. (Finding a phone and calling long distance from Michigan to Forest Hills, Queens in 1976 was easier said than done.)

      "Hello. It's me. You'll never guess who just I saw. I saw *Borges*."

      "Borges? What's a Borges?"

"*Borges.* He is the most important figure in modern literature. He influenced everyone. He is the father of pomo."
This rendition of the conversation is not verbatim. "Pomo" was probably not then used to stand for postmodernism. But I am sure that I am relaying a tape recorder perfect version of the rest of the phone call.
"Borges is a man? You are enraptured with Borges? Wonderful! Marry Borges!"
"I can't marry Borges. Borges is seventy-seven. I'm twenty-three. Borges is too old for me."
"Does Borges have a grandson?"
Having survived hearing this question, I went on to pursue further graduate work at SUNY Buffalo where I had the honor of studying with Leslie Fiedler. I never told my mother about how highly I regarded my chance personally to know Leslie. (No one ever called him Professor Fiedler.) Even though Leslie was old enough to be my father rather than my grandfather and he was married to his second wife and had many my age children, Leslie was *Jewish.* My mother never had the chance to hamper my graduate school career by appearing in Samuel Clemens Hall armed with a divorce lawyer and a rabbi named Marryin' Sam.
I am venturing into the way back machine because my memories about Borges and Fiedler—and enjoying an academic career marked by engaging with many famous authors and scholars—are symptomatic of my related and present day regret, a regret located in a galaxy far far away from my mother's purview. She triumphed in her world. She invited her Julia Richman High School classmate Lauren Bacall to my grandparents' upper west side apartment. Because she thought that he had talent, she told her friends to listen to a then unknown singer named Frank Sinatra. She received personal

letters from Tyrone Power. I, in contrast, had never met Marshall McLuhan.

I am absolutely determined to rectify this situation. Okay, I know that it is December 2012 and Marshall McLuhan has not been with us since 1980. I am not going to let this small detail stop me. I am, after all, my mother's daughter. Nothing ever stopped her. She had the audacity to say "look at all of these women getting married why aren't you getting married?" when I was finally—at age forty-six—standing in front of a justice of the peace getting married in Queens Borough Hall. This fact did not deter the woman who incessantly, since the moment I was born, told me to get married. She never adhered to the tenets of the reality community. Why should I? She was the person I could best turn to when contemplating how to thwart chronological reality and meet McLuhan.
Positioning my closet as some Narnia-esque portal, I reached up to the highest shelf and retrieved the pile of letters Tyrone Power wrote to Miss Roslyn Diamond. With a slow and deliberate motion appropriate to Ouija board use, I ran her diamond wedding ring over Power's signature. .

"Tyrone. Tyrone Power. How can I have the power to speak with Marshall McLuhan?" I asked.

And then, lo, the key to the power became diamond crystal clear. The academic real world could never provide the solution. I could not introduce myself to McLuhan at, say, a Media Ecology conference. Only a method which combined my mother's attention to movie stars with my career-long dedication to science fiction's textual stars would provide the means for me to achieve my goal. It was time to merge the magic of Hollywood movies with fiction's unreality.

I sat in my living room surrounded by a circle consisting of Rozie's 1960's movie magazines and

Marleen Barr

1930's movie star scrapbook and Marleen's science fiction novels and scholarly journals. Texts pertaining to, for example, science fiction notables Darko Suvin and Samuel Delany were uncharacteristically included with descriptions of Liz and Dick and Jeanette McDonald and Nelson Eddie. (Once upon a real time, my mother's hopes were dashed. After I let her know that "Chip" Delany once said "Marleen I love you" in public, I added that he is famously gay.) And so, ensconced within the Rozie/Marleen special interest circle, I began to try to resurrect McLuhan. My version of "resurrect" is not too *goyische*. I am very blunt: "Oy, Marshall McLuhan would you please appear now immediately if not sooner," I chanted earnestly. Nothing happened. I threw in some magic words. "The medium is the message," I fruitlessly shouted. "Global village" didn't work either. Like a fairy tale protagonist, I tried "hot media" and "cool media." Both of these terms failed to be just right.

It was time to incorporate some heavy duty textuality. I opened the July 2006 volume of *Socialism and Democracy* and turned to my article called "Science Fiction and the Cultural Logic of Early Post Postmodernism." I transformed what I had written about McLuhan into the following incantation:

> What would Marshall McLuhan say [about the JetBlue plane passengers who, in September 2005, watched their circling and potentially crashing plane on their seat back television screens]? McLuhan might say that the Global Village includes the stratosphere: both airborne and earth-bound viewers enjoyed equal access to the same 'cool media' cable anchor data-filled commentary. 'The medium is the message' is most applicable to the JetBlue incident in terms

of post postmodernism, however. As McLuhan explains, the 'effects of technology do not occur at the level of opinions or concepts, but alter sense ratios or patterns of perception steadily and without any resistance' [*Understanding Media: The Extensions of Man*]. . . . So much for what McLuhan might say. I say that McLuhan provides a basis for my claim that the JetBlue incident . . . epitomizes post postmodernism.

To make a long story about a long quotation short, citing my own words about McLuhan failed to cause him to materialize. Ditto for quoting McLuhan himself. I was, however, making progress. The young graduate student Marleen who saw Borges did not write post pomo metafiction. Not so for moi Marleen who has just put her criticism into her fiction. (Don't ask me to explain this point. This is a story, not a critical article. Oy, I'm having enough trouble trying to talk to McLuhan. Don't even think about requiring me to analyze this story. "Fawgetaboutit.")

It was time to pack in the Ouija board approach and go back to the drawing board. As I was reverently putting Rozie's movie memorabilia back on their closet shelf location, I began to think about the implications of having a mother who incessantly behaved like a Woody Allen film protagonist. And then it hit me: Allen could provide the means for me to schmooze with McLuhan. When teaching Introduction to Media Theory, I always show my students the clip of McLuhan's cameo appearance in *Annie Hall*. Every time I play the clip, I wish that I could enter the movie and engage with McLuhan. Allen, in *The Purple Rose of Cairo*, pictured a version of my wish coming true. He portrays movie character Tom Baxter jumping out of the film frame to interact with a real world person named Cecilia. If Cecilia can talk to filmic Tom, then why can't Marleen talk to filmic Marshall?

All I had to do was to figure out a way to inveigle myself within *Annie Hall.* How? Well, I could channel my inner Barbra Streisand starring in *Yentl.* I thought about falsely presenting myself as a male rabbi via donning a big black hat and a long black coat and taping *payesses* to my head. This disguise would enable me to hide out in the *Annie Hall* Midwestern *goyim* dinner eating family closely encountering a New York Jew scene. I had to reject this tactic. McLuhan did not appear in the dinner scene. I could possibly get lost forever in a 1977 Allen film. And then I would never get married! I had to find a way to enter *Annie Hall,* talk to McLuhan immediately, and get out fast. I had to consult an expert. I had to ask Tom Baxter.

Deciding that I needed to pick an auspicious day to attempt to pose my question to Baxter—i.e. it is logical for a Baby Boomer to go into "when the moon is in seventh house and Jupiter aligns with Mars" mode— I decided to make my attempt on 12/21/2012. I ordered *Purple Rose* from *Netflix.* When the film arrived, I loaded it into my giant flat screen television's DVD player. (I just had to tell Marshall about *Netflix* and giant flat screen televisions.) I pushed the "play" button. I looked directly at Baxter on the screen and earnestly stated my request.

"Hello Mr. Baxter. I would like to ask you a question. Would you please come out?"

And there he was standing in my living room. It was a miracle. You don't believe me? Well, I stated my request on Hanukah. McLuhan would say that television screen electric light is a technologically advanced version of oil lamp light. If an oil lamp light miracle happened once upon a time, it is perfectly sensible that a television screen light miracle could happen now. Adhere to what Coleridge called "the willing suspension of disbelief." Or, in McLuhan's words, "alter [your] sense ratios or patterns of perception steadily and without any resistance." Resistance is futile; the medium is the message.

Sensing that time could be of the essence, I immediately explained my objective to Baxter.

"I want to go inside *Annie Hall* so that I can speak to Marshall McLuhan. You are quite adroit at moving in and out of a Woody Allen movie. Please tell me what I should do," I said while hoping that he would not ask me to secure a broom, follow a yellow brick road, or deal with a tornado. I had had enough *tsuris* coping with traversing blacked out streets and cleaning up vis-à-vis Hurricane Sandy.

"First, you must identify your own version of the purple rose of Cairo."

"But I am a native New Yorker. I don't know anything about botany. My only experience of Egypt is the 'you shouldn't know from it' slavery depicted in the *Haggadah*."

"Think. Make a purple rose your own. You can substitute any location for Cairo."

"Well, Rose Modell is the only Rose I know. She was my paternal grandmother's cousin and she was married to Henry Modell, the CEO of Modell's Sporting Goods Stores. I will never forget Rose and Henry. When I was nine, my mother introduced me to them because she wanted me eventually to marry one of their grandsons. I know that you are neither female nor human nor Jewish. But can you imagine what it was like to have a Jewish mother who was *mashuganah* about arranging for me to marry a rich Jewish husband to the extent that she wanted to sell me to a Modell's mogul?"

"No, I really do not understand. But what matters is that Rose Modell was very important to *you*. Just figure out how to make her purple and locate her where you wish."

I opened my parents' wedding album and removed the picture of Rose and Henry toasting my newly married parents at their 1949 St. Moritz Hotel wedding reception. I xeroxed the picture using my computer scanner and, with marking pen in hand, painted Rose's face purple.

"Here is my purple Rose. She lived in Sheepshead Bay. Would the purple Rose of Brooklyn work?"

"Absolutely."

"So what do I do now?"

"Wait for an auspicious day. Watch *Annie Hall*. Stop the film on the McLuhan scene. Think lovely McLuhanesque scholarly thoughts. Wave your purple Rose of Brooklyn picture. Hope for the best. Jump in."

"This idea definitely will not fly. What about the television's glass? I can't jump through glass. If the shards don't kill me, my husband will for breaking the television. I can't do a Cinderella fairy tale mirror mirror on the wall thing. It won't apply to me. Cinderella was a *shiksa*."

"All I can tell you is that you must do all that you can to make the experience your own. I have nothing else to say. Good-bye Marleen. It was nice to meet you."

I waited for December 21, 2012, the day the world was supposed to end via Planet X/Nibiru generated Mayan apocalypse. Well, in case the apocalypse was not apocryphal, I had nothing to lose. But, as a science fiction scholar who did not believe that Planet X/Nibiru would do Earth in, I had to take every precaution to mitigate against death by glass shard. So, I turned to Neil Gabler's *Life The Movie: How Enter-*

tainment Conquered Reality. Gabler uses the term "behind the glass" to describe the space located inside television screens. I had to conquer reality to venture there. His book was tailor made for my situation. Media theory could not fail me in my quest to meet McLuhan.

Clutching both my purple Rose of Brooklyn picture and *Life The Movie*, I held my breath, prayed to Planet X/Nibiru (even though praying to a potential Mayan apocalypse now planet is not Jewish, I needed all the help I could get), and hurled myself against the television glass. I did not think that I was in 2012 New York anymore. Because there he was. I was face to face with a tall stately figure with thinning hair wearing a light colored sports jacket.

"Professor McLuhan. I love your work. I have always regretted never having met you. But as a pioneering feminist science fiction scholar, I like to think that I have spent my life walking along the ground breaking academic trail you blazed. I met your University of Toronto colleague Clark Kent at a Media Ecology conference held at Fordham University. He described the warring factions in the Toronto English department and said that your professional enemies gave you *tsuris* from hell. But, in the end, you triumphed. You make me feel that despite all professional torpedoes, it is necessary to remain true to one's scholarly beliefs and forge full speed ahead. Thank you, Professor McLuhan. Thank you for the earth shatteringly original scholarly ideas you gave to the world. Thank you, thank you from my heart, for serving as a role model to me. And, last but not least, I must tell you about the present world's giant flat screen televisions and *Netflix*. And cellphones, the 'communicators' Captain Kirk routinely used, are pervasive. I love how you said that '[w]e live science fiction.' You were so right. You were right about everything. Thank you!"

"You are most welcome. It was a pleasure to meet you, Marleen," said McLuhan as he disappeared within a puff of smoke.

I opened my window to dissipate the smoke. I saw a giant bleached blonde female head encompassing the entire top of the Empire State Building. I had somehow entered another Woody Allen movie: *New York Stories*, Marleen version. The giant Jewish mother's all-encompassing head belonged to Rozie. I had to tell her my latest news.

"I just met McLuhan."

"McLuhan? What's a McLuhan?"

"No, I am not going there. McLuhan is dead. You're dead. If you tell me to marry McLuhan, I will die."

"It is not necessary for you to marry McLuhan. You are already successfully married. Okay, your husband is not Jewish—but, since you got married at forty-six, I had to look away. Mazel tov. I am happy with you."

Rozie was happy with me at long last? I fainted from the shock.

I woke up in my living room and saw my husband watching our perfectly intact television.

"Why are there small pieces of glass in front of the television?" he asked. "And why are you *schwitzing*?"

"Even though I taught you some Yiddish, you will never comprehend how the glass shards got in here. Since the world is supposed to end today, perhaps there is something askew in the space/time continuum. In other words, ya shouldn't know from it. Or just chalk it up to what will always remain unknowable to you, what you would call a 'Jewish thing.' Just think that the glass relates to an ancient Jewish ritual involving breaking a glass at weddings."

Marleen Barr

My husband, ever ready to tune out all that is Jewish, calmly directed his attention back to his television program. In the manner of *The Twilight Zone* closing verbiage, control of the television set returned to normal. Frank Sinatra, sans any media technology, began to sing *New York, New York*. Rozie was *kibitzing* with Frank and Tyrone—and Jorge Luis and Marshall.

Why did I hear my own personal live Sinatra concert on December 21, 2012? I repeat: Rozie was one of the first people to notice and acknowledge Frank's talent. She always did it her way. He owed her one.

McLuhan, Arthur Asa Berger

Mary Ann Allison

McLuhan Kaleidoscope

Immersed in the global village,
    in a circus of messages,

      blessed and beguiled,
      so much magic everywhere,
          if (If) we're lucky,   we
                            hear the huckster;

we listen to

    a backward barker, McLuhan,
          McLuhan, draws us in   to
                        draw us out.
  shows us

                      (He's hard
    the gaps   to hear. So little signal;
    the holes, the   so much noise.)
  holes in our lives,
the electrical loneliness,
            the isolation of too many symbols,
                too little flesh.

With a whiff of popcorn, the smile of a pop culture icon,
      a hint of Roman Catholic incense,
      the pain of an outcast academic,

McLuhan shows us the   disconnections in
                                connections.

Mary Ann Allison

When,   long ago (so twentieth century),

when this   scholar,
        this   pop culture circus barker,
        this   magician,
                looked into our world,

    all the layers of media,
    all the levels of abstraction,
        floated, formed, crystallized,

                broke apart;
when he looked,
when McLuhan looked,

    all the layers of media,
    all the levels of abstraction,

        floated,
(quite astonishing;   formed again, but,
  Schrödinger's cat, neither alive nor dead)   in his seeing,
        did not freeze, and

    formed   again,   in his seeing,
        and again,   as he needed,

                as we needed.

        Long dead, living now,

    living now through his printed words,

scholar McLuhan,
barker McLuhan,   draws us in,
        gives us   a carnival gift,

Mary Ann Allison

                    a child's toy,
        full of illusion,   cardboard and plastic:
        from cheap beads   and mirrors,

    symmetric patterns:

a kaleidoscope,   a way   of seeing,
                            of seeing patterns,
                            of seeing media patterns.

                            Take a breath;
turn the flimsy cardboard ring at the end,
                                see the magic.

  This bead,   echoed over and over,
        connects me to those I love   no matter where.
  This bead   shows my parents' love letters,
      love reflected   over and over.
  This bead,   jitters and jutters,   multiple
      messages mirrored,   seismic shocks, meaning
                      shatters.

  This bead, ah, this bead: though obsolete,
      nothing is lost. History,   learned or
                        unlearned, is
    reflected, remediated, or
    repeated   over   and over.

It grows dark;
    after all,   it has been
                              hours,
            ages,
       since Toto pulled the curtain back;

      evening comes,
   (media) epochs end;

Mary Ann Allison

       the circus tents are folded,
       the wizard retreats   to Kansas (or Toronto).
                                    Even so,
even so,

new beads,   in the old kaleidoscope,
new beads,   in
             in the old,   the old kaleidoscope,

new beads,   new beads,

reflect all the old   reflect all the new
            connects and   connects and
              disconnects.   disconnects.

      In the magic reflections of McLuhan's old,
                          new kaleidoscope,

in the beads of new messages,   refracted and reflected,
                      repeated and remediated,

                        we can see,
      (as the beads shift)   we can hear,

                 that   we create,
                 that   we are

            messages of   ourselves   and the

                  (now) universal village.

Blocks, Dean Motter

John McDaid

Flash in the Pan

It's easier out at sea when they bury you
Here in the Western World they're just gonna carry you
Into some marble room where they can worship you
For being at last without mind
Just another flash in the pan
Just another mind in a cage
Just another 2000 Man
Just another product of the age
Walking down the street snared up in Indra's net
Trying to make enough to keep all the monsters
out of my head
Trying to keep up a little with all those books I read
Don't make no difference now what Plato said
Just another flash in the pan
Just another mind in the cave
Just another 2000-year-old scam
Just another Nobly Lied-to slave
Working in the air-conditioned office,
talking on the phone
To all the target demographics undercover back home
Drawing conclusions on the bathroom wall,
cowering under your desk
Staring out the window at the concrete wilderness
– You can be my guest, cuz I'm
Living in a world of make believe
What does it enhance? What does it obsolesce?
What does it retrieve?
It reverses into the world to be taken as real
At the speed of light phenomenology
gets a pretty raw deal
Just another flash in the pan
Just another mind in a cage

John McDaid

Just another 2000 man
Just another product of the age
Broken on the wheel of temporal causality
The telephone pole of information replaced
the wisdom of the tree
Sipping tea sitting by the radiator, waiting for the mail
You know that plain brown wrapper
just might contain the Holy Grail
– It never fails, cuz I'm
Stuck in this wetware network of on-off gates
Trying to find a way to cross over
into some altered states
Thinking about the latest transmission from the Beast
She said you know there ain't no way back from that
Journey to the East
Just another flash in the pan
Just another mind in a cage
Just another 2000 man
Just another product of the age

Tony Burgess

Start

It is hard to control her broken arm from the outset. The moment the bone ~in question~ uncuffed(?) we were beset with a distracting list ~of questions~. The first ~in question ~and the second ~of questions~. . The girl ~in question ~had broken her arm in a film and so it was instructive: however when we set the bone and she fainted we set in motion a series of HOME. The arm it turned out was always going to be broken in the film and we were always going to be not fixing it. From this ~in question~ sprang the new natured ~of questions~ and, like a thick terrible cast – or pause tunnel – or tube frame – appeared the portmanteau – uncuffed. It is hard to commence a series of HOME at the outset.

Stephen Roxborough

dear marshall i know you

don't care how many letters i have
after my name or if the galaxy is spiraling out of control
or not
because i know the difference between stories
round the campfire & a fireside radio chat
letting go by watching the river flow
& escaping the world in a novel
shakespeare's stage & demille's epic technicolor
the world wide web & network programming
the convenient inconvenience of hand helds
& promethian jumbotrons
so pervasive & stupifying i wonder
are we watching godless screens
or are they watching us?

i revel in the difference between a QE2 crossing
& supersonic flight armstrong's hot 5 & miles davis'
birth of the cool monet's soft focus
kandinsky's chaos & pollack's spattered
oozing universe babe ruth & muhammed ali
frank sinatra & michael jackson
emily dickenson & margaret mead
the dalai lama & the pope mickey mouse & bart simpson
mary pickford & marilyn monroe bill bissett
& george bowering winnie the pooh & harry potter
venus & mars beatles & the stones
marie antoinette & annette funicello
benjamin franklin & bucky fuller
adolf hitler chairman mao & osama bin laden
john d. rockefeller & donald trump
joan of arc & jane fonda

Stephen Roxborough

ted turner & rupert murdock
george orwell & king george the third
jules vern & arthur c. clarke
1984 & 2001 it takes a cosmos
to raise a global village

i celebrate the difference between the front page
& the funny pages conservative & liberal
fanzines punkzines teenzines & e-zines
60 30 & 15 second spots
45s 78s LPs CDs & MP3s
law boards draftboards sandwich boards billboards
& T-shirts
hardcover paperback chapbook facebook
bookmarking comic books holybooks & e-books
NFL NHL NBA & MLB
a simple cuppa joe & grande latte madness
gold watches & severance packages
HBO & GMO paper or plastic newton & quantum
vietnam conflict & the gulf war tricky dick
& barack obama rainbow warriors & the corporate
peacock
rallies protests marches sit-ins strikes
occupy wall street & middle east occupations
black holes wormholes & further down the rabbit holes
is anything still sacred
or has profane swallowed us whole?

i celebrate the media electric
sift through the difference between docudrama
& reality TV channel surfing mindsurfing
bodysurfing & internet surfing save the whales
& climate change
IBM & apple forbidden fruit
from the last withering tree of knowledge
rocket boosters & search engines

Stephen Roxborough

second life first
blogs vlogs grog spaceship logs & lost in cyberspace
snailmail email junk mail & spam the grand
ole opry & magic echos from max yasgur's farm
amazon google youtube & yahoo
flash floods & flash mobs
breaking news & broken truth
text & twitter history & hearsay
AM FM PM & PMS
everyone's infected everything's connected
hot flashes cool mashes warm washes
red green black & blue
sunrise rainbow sunset & glow
in the dark
the wheel the tribe the globe
our family the galaxy
a round & around all comes & goes
round you & me
and i know dear marshall
whatever medium you're in now
you know too because you
always saw the bigger picture
& the picture bigger
times two

Lillian Allen

Marshalling McLuhan

*"We look at the present through a rear view mirror.
We march backwards into the future." – Marshall McLuhan*

"The missing link created far more interest than all the
chains and explanations of being."
The oldest voice in the world is only the beginning
The youngest is you, eye shape-shifting back to silence
The question that multiplies meaning
Chants charted, storm center whirlwind, words
The poet intones them, Howl.
Ah Ruba-dub Stylee Rant -ing The Arugula Fugues
Tweets the corpus of the mundane
Trivium (con)texted
What disappears evades the gaze
We are the analogue of spirit
Echoes reflect refracting
The earth is water and stone and wonder
Hoomei percussive winds swirling among rocks
Moving from the silence from the nothingness
Through the sound world to take shape
Lock sight into visual space
Keying into position, as if words can be
Separate or separated from language
And language from culture
And culture from kin
Narrative and myth are the threads,
Jesus, Cayote, Anancy
The world of presence entered
by Africa's eponymous beat
Trap drums snare the Congo Basin
rattles for the Amazon Rain Forest
in the rear view; Pimachiown Aki

Lillian Allen

One world rippling to the next
Borders of sounds and sense, light quantize
Vibrations intermingling
Breath, squawks, squeaks, gulps
Wirelessly wired body snatching
This ring tones invasion
Just when did God say; "Let there be cell phones"
If the times are modern, is the spirit modern?
Or must it lumber through the black-hole
with old clothes on its back?
Steve Jobs now cavorting with Moses

Comparing Tablets?
Was it not Moses' voice rippling through
Steve Jobs' last breath?
oh wow, wow, wow
The Circuited City, electrical to the brain
Synapses snap fracking words
Reverberating new worlds
A digital bix flick, clicks
Nirvana in the lawnmower's sputt sputt
To contemplate the algorithms of the digital after-life
Equation of how many taps on a keyboard
To tap tap into the over-life, a simple typo "o"
---Oh my
"Good? or God? the newly crossed-over asks
Totality is not possible
A few taps we are from infinity
This keyboard in nano life
There are no closed systems
It's all an illusion
Reality the etchings of spirit, one small dimension
Electrical messages mixing meshing connecting
The digits we are
Tap tap tapping
Politicians are the new advertisers

Lillian Allen

They have monopolized it all;
the locutionary act, the illocutionary act,
the prelocutionary act. All act. Hollywood's art
Even objectivity is an illusion
From the black-hole, thoughts form themselves
Mere digits, impulse to move us to wonder
like organically growing things, exponential
and the subjective eye
to rebel and revel in images we hold onto
like we can know the world
Remembering
Does it really matter
if it's Shakespeare or Edward deVere?
Somewhere in the uni-verse Shakespeare&deVere
are one-and-the-same
just rippling through w—a—t—e---r
Or in the multi-versal, they're a dime-a-dozen
More plentiful than a spoken-word poet's bravado.

Peter Montgomery

Life

We live as if we were forever
riding
backwards on the stallion.
Centaur, mute mutant

We see the field
Awash with the past.
The future is a twist around.
Too hard to keep in focus.

Nothing to say.

Adeena Karasick

Messy Necessity

Invention is the mother mére moré amoré of necessity
the lover of necessity
incessantly messy in the recessed precipice recipes

re-inventing, *avanting*
in the suture the rapture, aperture of necessity
the saucy ipseity

in the pétite plais very berry pluparfait, polyplaited plumerais
of a wrangled anglais

dropping its MOTHERLOAD
in the *imma. mäter madré mére, mer/*sea *MERCI !*

of swirling necessity

in the re-assessed fest of cresting necessity
hoochie mama of invested necessity
chimera mere myriad
of messy necessity

and is gettin' all
tribal: and *up in your*
business

like a technomediatic sticky sprecht striptease --

whose DEW line, a low lying fault line,
a misaligned freulein

whose HOT PRINT

Adeena Karasick

is burning; through
the technology of its letters --

all sibilant and sweaty
in the misc-en-scene-ey
panacea polyplotted plumerais

because invention was just
BORN THIS WAY

and is kneeling at your feet
undressing itself before you

with its neo-psychedelic, post-apocalyptic
blogzilla buzz of its backlash / electric hashtag
flashing you

with its intergalactically-studded arcana

in the imagined pageantry
of all that is ravenous and cavernous and
dripping with *cool media*

en medias massaging its oratoric sensorium re-storied in
        riddled middles modes
    spilling its codes loading its nodes

is a mother

of necessity

fanning its transom
pinching its poesie
messaging it medium

Adeena Karasick

(and in the son sequitur récriture)
is a ****MOTHERPLUCKER**** (of necessity)

                                              all hot n lingual

romancing the drama of
necessity all lingually messy
and ripe
with the architecture
of moist reverence.

Adeena Karasick

In My Blogal Village, Print is Hot

Writing in a time in which the city was breaking down under the impact of suburban growth and dispersion, and was rapidly becoming obsolete, Marshall McLuhan, repainted the world as a polyglossic multimedic hyperlinked conglomerate. Everything conflagrated in a gigantic intergalactic technologic nervous system.

> *These new media of ours ... have made our world into a single unit....the world is now like a continually sounding tribal drum, where everybody gets the message.... all the time. A princess gets married in England and boom boom boom go the drums and we all hear about it; an earthquake in North Africa, a Hollywood star gets drunk...away go the drums again. I use the word tribal....it is probably the key word ...* (McLuhan, 1960)

50 years later not much has changed:
A sapphire-studded party-planner princess
gets married in England.
A tsunami happens in Japan.
A Hollywood starlet powders her nose.

Our lives have become a kind of carnivalesque intertextilic journey where every moment, a wriggling insignia of angles, codes, references, concentrated emanations and transmutations. And the city itself has become a multiplatform interdisciplinary repository; an archive of fragments, updates, analysis, aggregates, advice.

Adeena Karasick

The question is no longer about urban development but inhabiting a webbed network of serial simultaneity enfolding in on itself; neo-formalized fragments of post-consumerist media-infused culture.

A culture where television (as an interlinked totality) *is everywhere.*
A culture where Print is HOT

And I couldn't agree more, (in *my* city) **PRINT IS HOT**

And not only is it HOT, but (according to 12th century Kabbalist, Isaac the Blind of Provence, "contains the *whole* universe and all the future creations"), the dense matter of the Big Bang spewing out its definitions and associations of light into the void. There *is* nothing outside of it / no beginning, end or containment but all is illocatable in a locus of interlocution; a diology of drifts and divergence, disintegration and desire.

And i look around now and I see
print *and* media. we text with our phones and call with our computers
I see screens. Everywhere. (Cool. COOL media --)

On fridges and microwaves, in bedrooms and park benches. Screens, in your lap, in your face, on gas pumps grocery stores and airplanes. In Times Square, Yonge Street screens on table tops n subway stops, and we, gently stroking them, big screens, little screens, flat screens and LEDs; windows; portals into new cities of being. -- where you can mash up and LIVE inside language; literally inside tv film video phones and podcasts, inside music and video poems, email and blogs books that merge text and images all layered-up and transmediatic lexicons of bissett Borges Baudelaire Baudrillard, the contemporary financial meltdown, semiotic theory; fuzzy science and post-apocalyptic Gutenbergian globalization, The Arab Spring, London Riots, Occupy Wall Street – *And it may be melting the world, because*

It's hot.

And as meaning splits, gathers and re-disseminates and all that is written and all that is performed, imaged, youtubed, twittered and tagged emerges as one text, a vortext of memes, appellations, inscription and silences.

And, just as meaning forms and reforms through the constant transformation of language, my city, my community forms and reforms around me, including me, excluding me, nomadic communities of constant change, renewal and obliteration. Technology lets me live in New York, shop in Montreal, commune in Paris, sell in Frankfurt, sun in Greece, work in Chennai through planes, trains, boats, buses, modems, hyper-links, skypes and pay gateways always Searching, ever Searching through the ever denser vocabulary of information that surrounds and envelopes us.

It's Hot
And it's Cool
It's in and it's out. It's up and it's down

It's a media frenzy where print and image are conflagrated and erupt in a hyperlinked midrashic-infused, post-literate anti-consumerist, hyper-generative aesthetics highlighting

A global village that localizes.

Adeena Karasick

A BLOGAL VILLAGE
of conflated borders, (deflated borders, bankrupt
Borders) that reborder in *deborder*, excess

Its locus in language

A Hot language

an echonomimesis poiesis, a cross-pollination of genre
and media coupled with transgressive linguistic
practices. Maintaining that it's not that books (á la The
Gutenberg Galaxy) are responsible for most of the ills of
modern society; nationalism, war, industrialization,
population explosion, the breakdown of human
relations in urbanized chaos—but *how* you read them,
where you read them.
One need interact *with* the book.
For, it is not "sharp in definition, filled with data,
exclusively visual and verbal, psychologically damaging
and low in audience participation."

But whether on a page or on a screen it is infinitely
expandable touchable recs/citable.

DEMANDING AUDIENCE PARTICIPATION

And when my city is my screen, I am fully involved
with my PRINT, texting my youtubed tumblr twitter
while facebooking my foursquare hopstoppin'
techniverse

My reading is always a process of transformation,
metamorphosis, substitution, deformation.

My Print is Hot.

Adeena Karasick

Hot and difficult. It is highly syntactic, grammatical and demands a high level intellectual activity; operates with an elevated linguistic intensity, is marked by textual irregularities and may cause initial withdrawal because it may not be immediately available. It's got poor adaptability, is marked with sensory overload and can cause extreme emotions.

IT IS HOT
and is reveling in its own miasma.
Fashioning and refashioning
And becomes part of the cultural fabric.
It IS my cityscape

and demands interaction

(For i read the city and city reads me)

And so it's crucial to remember that it's not just the transcendental or cultural or historical or ideological or psychoanalytic deduction of a work but how it plays out; one's interaction with it, its performance ---

So, it's not just the "t-t-t-t-telephone",
modern painting, and television
(all "electric and oral-auditory, tactile, and visceral")
that highlights a sense of connectivity, but

i inhale my print, feel it against my skin, on my tongue in my throat, engage with it. Viscerally, actively with every breath of my body, i taste each letter

And *this,* the mother of neces **sity**
A lingually messy city
Of synchronicity, historicity, reciprocity
And cannot escape it.

Adeena Karasick

So even though I find *this* particular binaric opposition frustrating, what *is* clear is that the world *is* rapidly becoming a *global village*, in which we communicate in a super modern version of the way tribal societies were once related. But, it's not through an overthrow of typographic and literate communications (with its seamless web of kinship and interdependence.)

But an inclusion of text *and* image. A merging of the oral, the written, the encrypted and performed; all that is sacred, grotesque and graphematic. And it *is* everywhere.

Now, I live in New York City and am continually bombarded with what's outside, inside re-sited in a scite of excess and desire, consumption, re-sited in infinite translation. Re-fertilized with every look, gaze, panoptically re-creating its own borders, orders, limits, laws, flaws / forging its own auto-correcting tribalism

The city is alive, inside its language.
all twittering and blogoscopic

low-lying and high-def. The television is everywhere
My city is my screen.
My locus in language. On iPods, Pads smart phones.

And I take in my city: A village of COOL IMAGES and HOT PRINT.

All webbed up and buttoned down,
intratextual and hyperlinked

It is an intra-galactic lexical plexus
of screening media

Adeena Karasick

a misc-en-sceney panacea

cannibalizing itself through its own lateral feed nodes,
all mythinformed and tweety
like a chatroulette stalker
sucking on its own
saucy posturing of
geographies of content

And as McLuhan (as urban prophet visionary saw)

"The answers are always inside the problem,
not outside".

And like knowledge itself, "expands exponentially".

And we are now living [*ne pas de hors text*], in a
technomediatic vortext --
with no core text
a "global" assemblage
where my APP is bigger than your APP
And we are living

on the edge, the edge the edge the edge the edge
[Lady Gaga]

of all that is hot *and* cold,

full of print *and* media. All that is urban and suburban
and global and all that is tribal, rivaled, malleable,
saleable, viable

And through all that is twittered and youtubed
foursquared and flickred

i am

Adeena Karasick

hanging on a moment with you

in an infinitely shifting screen of urban suburbia
comprised of a globalatti of illicit tribalism; living
somewhere between my 144 characters, interactive
e-books, googley-eyes and tricked tweets, my city
is a telemediatic global village

where Print is hot. So hot its burning through its own
platform; setting my screen on fire. Through a hyper-
linked interactive mode of desire and webbed linkages
of interaction and connexion, insurrection, reflection
ideolection suspension,

My PRINT IS HOT

Foraging in a village that exceeds spatiality, locality,
dimension.

Temporally and graphically ever-expansive,
where my cityscape, a *lang'scape* inseparable from the
media that expresses it.

So, it's not *just* that "The Media is the Message,"

but *en medias*
IS THE MESSAGE

In the middle of things. And this *message* never begins
ab ovo, ad initio but *en medias.* In an "excluded mid-
dle" of conflict flashbacks, references, journeys, modes
mid points looking ahead, looking back, sideway
through dramatic webs of relations

-- *I AM MESSAGING MY MEDIUM* ---

Adeena Karasick

massaging my language which is
creating its own urbanity

So, in this age of google-obsessed twitter tinged trickled tweets of post-literary construction, *what is the cityscape?* Whether it's weaving an intertextilic lexicon, a web of contradictory discourses or using technology to insert itself into, and explode traditional ideology concerning the locus of the book,

"we [are looking] at the present through a rear view mirror. We march backwards into the future". We see that the future is always a-coming, *en arrivant,* arriving, *la-venir,* is always coming and arriving *from* itself; engages in a process of production inscribed between promise and promiscuity; re passed in a repast of a past of re-passed postulates

and whether the text is *on* the page, or a pageantry of cellphones, kindles, readers videos, computer screens iTouching their way through a post-literary technoversive generation of *iteration;* dissemination and creation

There is *Hot Print in the City*
(running wild and lookin' pretty)

expanding and contracting;
infinitely re-forming.

Re-framing the village.

Adeena Karasick

Your Leaky Day

"The Future Leaks Out" - Marshall McLuhan

There is leaking at the Sheremeteyevo airport, leaking
in the Sinai, striking leaks in Syria
oh memory and meaning are leaking
live, and on the *Egged* bus to *Bet Shemesh*
there is leaking among the letters
But you cannot take a leak.

And as Gertrude Stein might say,
a liking is a leaking and as leak likes like in like eyes
in a creek of tweeted leaks,
we're up all nite to get leaky.

like a freaky leak, at a late-nite leak easy
peeky leaks, trick-or-treaty leaks
midnite-quickie leaks

Hey sweet leaks,
In the Rape of the Leak or on the banks of plumb
leak, how do leased leaks look
through the leaking glass?

And as the future leaks out
like an Angel of history, in the sink time,
oh hero stay steadfast through night's back--
60,000 leaks under the sea struts the shocks are leaking

as time leaks and truth flies hungry leaking
between the lines of the story when my name is leak
cause there's a leak in this old building
a leak at the disco a leak like a body

So when you're down on your leak, it's just

the leak of the draw. Don't give me a dirty leak –

in a ratcheted-up snack pack of tweaked leaks
a leak of extraordinary gentlemen
a leak *of their own*
of shadows and legends,
in a leaky boat, just leak

like a drowned rat, leak *lively*
and leak ahead.

As elite leaks look like a look-alike leak in the
happy-go-leaky Land-of-Leaks leaky streak, just leak
on the bright side or leak the other way

'cause all leakered up,

i'm leaking out my back door leaking
all leak-warm. My name is leaka and
i live on the 2nd floor, oh just leak at me i'm Sandra Dee
at the the Joy Leak Club
leaking so good on the dancefloor
leak closely now, *are you watching me now*
and just leak what you've done
through me to the sky, into the mirror --

wreaking or leaking *ichs*
all eked-out, leaking into it, things ARE
leaking up

EXCESS

sticky leaks
Sam-slick cheeky leaks or sleek chic leaks
Hula-girl tiki leaks

it's important to remember
the squeaky leak gets stirred

BW Powe

Reader

Come quietly with me
into silent letters again

fellow falling cipher
in the alphabet marking

 (they'll say the page is called
a dead tree medium)

come quietly with me
to decode the dust

in the speck
of a small word

how we could be
breaking through

Technogenie

Steve Jobs channeling the transit
into the ether

where we find resurrections
we know there are graves

*

Through apples and pads
pods and phones gods and goddesses
struggle to come become
reborn to be apocalypse everyday

I orbit with atoms
eons and nexus quivering
in photon momentum
the angular circuiting

i and i and i and i
this rapturous drive
electron expression
bodiless from molten ports

I'm inside a wireless angel-form
in kinetic mental migration
eternity's redacting attempt
to wake up in us

*

I hover and conceive the unthinkable invention
the implosive technology that will end

separation and lamentation tuning us
to the super-conscious connective soul
when infinity can go up for sale
on eBay while lineups lengthen at Futureshop
for the blues and reds that promote
overcoming our jelly pregnant gasp

*

Posh the body in the third eye of seasonless space
I hail you in the fluid heating
of your PC

occult sending what do you touch
on iScreen messaging someone not there
or here

you're hive-casting
into

        a live satellite

farewell old cracked self
exit ghost of anguish awareness
so long discrete being

welcome simulacrum
welcome android meme

rootless groundless
blackberry strew

anima overdrive

my voices are
              streaks
transferring through nerves

like dancers hopped up
on a hot clubbing night
hair-saloned in their strobing
lust for collagened lips

we're fast-FWDing
into shoreless bands
unlimited phonics optics
a battery of mind boosts

the pizzazz of increased being

                    *

But between the globe and the galaxy
I see with infrared eyes
a figure of a woman sliding by
white gowned guardian priestess
a slit in her dress dark-skin thighs exposed
and she turns in this reality she moves along
blessing my Eros with antique wisdom
she looks at me without opinion
how perfect her sidereal substance is
though she has no desire or hope
only a way of motioning peace
soothing my hardwired hunger to amaze

                    *

BW Powe

In holograms we wifi
you and I sphering the world like O2 moons
and whoosh abracadabra
transmitting transporting receive-conceive
into yin-yanging audio-global Ithaca light
you shadow you gust you uncanny molecular sea
you roll in innovators drones imagineers seers

all compatible systems of orchestrations
drink your elevations your weekends
your accounts your blood

why children say out of school
they're Harrys and Hermiones magi and avatars
prey pray to vampires and ghouls

*

With my master designer (Jonathan Ives
do you feel my IMs) we devise divinations
past the firewalls into the primordial intent

and EM flares on your retina skies
and VDT speed shapes ears and eyes

and insites quiver when you logon sensation
and you thinki am merging into empathy nets
and put your cursors on rotor with us

cloud of knowing
                       clouds of unknowing

I stream your sorrow
the brooding the body tomorrow and tomorrow
disappearing sweet earth goodbye

*

Static I'm losing you losing you
can you scan me
              breaking
up
into immaterial vision
(Walt Disney and Timothy Leary are alive)

static can you scope beyond cellular sleep
transiting into the spiritual deep

planet emergen-see
you input faster
emoticon icon
a hotspot a dot

tap the helter-skelter tongue
you bypass churches
faster for extreme mediation

in the veil of pixarmaking
your GPS-CGI singularity
              strings

kindlekind membrane

one breath one cell
one voice one brain
one day

William Marshe

(lang-gwij)?

what is
language
?

your illness.
your delicate torment
leaning against my open palm.
my quivering frustration
leaping between definitions.

where is
That word buried
for open fields;
their pale colours;
their wild and pale blooms
?

How do
They say
the rough ocean edge;
it's cool spray of breaking waves;
the smell of salty, drying kelp
beneath empty urchin shells
?

How can
They say
the hesitant, midsummer evening
dragging its drunken feet
over the threshold
of our inevitable horizon
?

William Marshe

      Where is
      That word
      ?
      Where is
      That house
      That word has built;
      That pit which grips
      That house
      ?

what is
language
?

That infinite space
which crawls
between my palm
and the timid skin of your suffering.

That wretched space
preventing my understanding
of your fading explanation
?

what is
language
    but useless.

what is
language
    other Than
    clandestine isolation
    ?

Steve Szewczok

Constitution of Silence

In here, there be what others fail to see, that, what has been built; What has been formed comes out of language itself. This structure of pauses and breath, causes that have had great effect, they have survived through Tens of Thousands of years.

A little time ago I found me near a friend who is close to my heart but distance having played it's part took me out of favor by speaking some words that were not of her flavor nor were they the kind of phrases that a friend dare speak to her gentle graces. I have to confess that I here did find myself under a great distress for never in good conscience would I, could I, displace whom I think of as grace herself; for I'm sure that word has her name on it, has her sustained upon it. I'm sure she is as Saint Mary was; a kind hearted mother, an instrument of goodness undiscovered.

I can see into the past. I can feel my way out this path by touching the cold wet rock, by rubbing the belly of this dark cave I am able to behave my way toward a light. What are we without it? How long could we survive without a Son or Daughter?

This morning I hear the bells of St. Mary's calling me: asking me to come to her; Come to her and remember, remember to worship and to pray with her in a quiet way, in a soundless and shy kind of way. Saint Mary and all of her kind speak to the mind of all who will listen. There be a great design here one that has had a movement for some two thousand years and here we are today, bells ringing, people singing, come and remember your history, your language, come and remember the words of the silent prayers and hear what they have to say.

Jill McGinn

we, the real mad poets

are not idealistic university students enamoured
with some wistful, romantic notion of madness
softly lit in the forgiving glow of candlelight,
starlight, moonlight blue slanted rays

we, one collective face of lunatic deviants
defy your christly catatonic categories,
have opted instead for allegories of oppression
we reject the thinly hidden xenophobia
sewn into the seams of your straightjacket jargon

we, the real mad poets chant and speak and sing aloud
in unison and diversity, we are storming your
Bastille of the psyche, eating your word salad
in the starvation of our poverty of affect

the medium is the message stands chanting
in the flesh,
the psycho speaking
is the poem

with our pressured speech we co-opt your
lexicon of pathology

with our clanging we transmute
our sick synesthesia into a synergy of mixed metaphor

we are committed to liberating a flight of ideas
into a heavenly revolution of doves
auditory hallucinations are cooing above
for the emancipation of words wrought to enslave

we, the real mad poets
are not going away

Phone, Dean Motter

Jerry Harp

Late Summer Twilight

Crows on balconies cry out, their calls
reaching into basements

where newspapers cover the walls, last centuries
advertisements, splashes

of light crossing the night sky, becoming
letters on a page,

banter for the boulevards. Look at the bright lights,
the colored lights, glass shards,

notes rising from musty schoolbooks that
could not hold them,

letters from a blank interior where the law becomes
flaws in the catalogue

and the land leaves off, no longer loam,
no longer auditory.

John Oughton

Pegged to Invisible Consequences

"Whatever happened to one particle would thus immediately affect the other particle, wherever in the universe it may be. Einstein called this 'spooky action at a distance'." – Amir D. Aczel

The most innocent words
entangle with things you would never particul-
arly expect: *bulrushes* binds to your lost love
Hazed excites tiny scurrying arthropods we are yet to
find on Mars
Even humble, transparent servant *the* is
one toy from childhood you still miss

Naturally, you suspect those words not yet disentangled
also have their allies, silent twins
Unrelated brain centers fire up in
haunted pinball game
flickering, chiming in a dusty arcade

At last we can argue progress
In the quantum mechanics of
uncanniness, perhaps poetry

David Batemen

McLuhan's Bride

once, at a graduate student soiree
the Professor's wife told me that McLuhan's wife
was afraid of her first vacuum cleaner

I was clearly shaken and hesitated to add that I
on the contrary, felt little techno based fear
when it came to small appliances
and all the strained emotional ties
they liberate their lovers from

and had, in fact, experienced a prolonged affair
late sixties
with my mother's first vacuum cleaner
an avocado Westinghouse
amply accommodating my great pubescent shaft
in a most delightful way

stored in the basement
this mechanical bride
this compact galaxy of carnal pleasure
pre-dating certain groundbreaking post-structuralist
thought
stood proud alongside boxes of old clothes, hunting
rifles
bewildered WWII army uniforms

my thoroughly modern fully equipped paramour
astute and wild-eyed in 'her' stolid ambient purring
giving me uncomplicated joy
strengthening my love for my mother
the ways in which she kept her house in order

David Batemen

supplying sons and lovers with
the necessary tools to survive
in a world where
as McLuhan claimed

"each of us lives several hundred years in a decade"

and

"when you are on the phone . . . you have no body"

inspiring one to think
when you are screwing a vacuum cleaner
you have no conscience, no need of one

      - save the sudden onset of a short circuit -

as you experience one pure act of
consummate industrial sel-indulgence
the grand sweep of history
in an age of information
that will one day go the way of

works of art, mechanical reproductions
items stored in a musty basement
boxes of old clothes, hunting rifles
bewildered WWII army uniforms
thoroughly modern fully equipped paramours
canisters astute and wild-eye-less
in their stolid ambient unplugged purring
having borne silent witness
to the great pubescent shaft of time

Michelle Anderson

The Mechanical Bride's Consolation

Taking up all the space above the fold on the front page of today's paper, directly underneath the newspaper's iconic Gothic-typed motto "Your Nose for News", was an advert of the ballet Luce wrote. Luce is my strange, estranged husband.

"The 'revolution' is intact," Luce is quoted as saying in the four-column interview, said, no doubt, while arching his eyebrow incredulously, wearing his usual look of a combination of deep consolation and surprise at having to explain it at all. "The story of Charlie McCarthy – title character and the sage of Waldorf Towers – brings Small Town America the freedom to listen, to read the book of the hour...to roast duck with Jefferson!"

I put the paper down, suddenly exhausted, next to two tickets to "Charlie McCarthy", Luce's ballet. "Crime does not pay," I say out loud. I'm in the kitchen of my home, alone, otherwise I would have said it silently, with know-how, with executive ability. Headed for failure, was more like it, in plain talk. The great books on Galluputians and media ecology, which I use in my market research work for Emily Post (she's my hero, and my boss), are on the table too, but what's on my mind is the ballet Luce wrote.

For my husband, for Luce, the co-education of the "poor" rich – those dead, white literary men of distinction with expertise on how not to offend – are not on his radar; only mine. The Era of Lil' Abner, Orphan Annie, even Bringing Up Father and Blondie, are Luce's to give the bold look to, from top to toe. Like Luce, I am boldly looking up to my son – a young man – and seeing the same reflection stare back at me. In the matter of my eye appeal, as a mother and as a woman in a mirror, both father and son see me the same way. It is my husband's choice; as a mother, I'm torn.

It used to be different. Luce, once upon a time, was, to me, the magic that changes mood and heart. I found his magic so profound that I believed the drowned man would un-drown at his touch. The voice of the lab, the scientist, would say that reality would say otherwise, and the truth is that I'm a product in his love-goddess assembly line, the mechanical bride with an expiration date, just one industrial unit in the folklore of Luce's isolated, illustrated success.

Superman, Tarzan… they're Luce's heroes, and herein lies a crack. Fictional characters with schemes and dreams, the corpse as still life, became real instead of just a picture he painted of our lives together. The great books, from Da Vinci to Holmes, lost their esteem in the matrimonial script the moment of our first breakfast at home. The mask came off, and he lost interest in understanding America, or me, for that matter, and what it means to have freedom – American style, with Cokes and cheesecake, labor strikes and bullet-proof vests.

To Luce I was a love novice, and it's true. I was. The law of the jungle, the education of "I'm Tough", having what it takes to stay in, or out, depending on who/what/when – I had no love experience. Until he came into my life screaming "Murder the umpire!" and "I am the Bill of Rights" like a lunatic to get my attention in the common room of the University where I studied the great books and Herbert Marshall McLuhan and Luce studied ballet, there was no twinkle that became our son.

Our son, my tough-as-Narcissus young man, appears suddenly in the kitchen, in front of me. I'm not alone in the house anymore. He looks down at me like Bogart's hero with that familiar look of complicated consolation. He looks down and I look up as a woman in a mirror, as a single line in a Pollyanna Digest, not as a mother.

"There's money in comics," says my son, picking up where he left off hours ago in his pitch to me for funding the purchase of rare Superman and Tarzan merchandise. At that moment, I make a decision.

Hours later:

In a corset, success.

Curve of fates, check.

Tickets and son, on board.

I watch as Luce's play unfolds the folklore of industrial man, woman and child, as told by the whirled sounds and sights of strings and brass and arms and legs. Horse opera and soap opera, it's all there. Phantasmagorical and obscene.

The woman playing me is gorgeous. I am strangely, deeply consoled.

Alexandra Oliver

Curriculum Vitae

"I may be wrong, but I'm never in doubt." - Marshall McLuhan

In '75, I drew the letter 'n'
Backwards, stapled Allison's left hand,
smoked Dad's last Montecristo, tore pell mell
through aisles on flights abroad (no matter where),
Yelled "poo!" in church, propelled a bag of bread
at someone's mother, piddled in the bed,
took a whack at cutting my own hair,
and ran away from Mum in some hotel
in Mexico. If dragged upon the stand,
I guarantee I'd do it all again.

In 1986, I went to meet
a boy who liked to carry a grenade,
crawled out the window to go and see the Cramps
while under curfew, peeled my own split ends,
set fire to Comet, lost my mother's ring,
complained when she was calm enough to sing,
wreaked havoc on my most enduring friends,
and broke a pair of ugly crystal lamps
in Hudson's Bay. If I could be remade,
I'd hit the switch which said, in red, REPEAT.

In '98, I drove a man to tears,
drank all night and jumped the subway stile,
not once, but twice. I snubbed the homeless, swore,
made eager interviewees ill-at-ease,
fought my secretary, spent paycheques
on underwear and hash for sloppy sex.
The hive of hell was crowded with my bees,
the sea of ill acquainted with my oar

Alexandra Oliver

but, asked if I would overwrite my file,
I'd walk away with cotton in my ears.

And now's the time to cast the vipers out,
sow sweetness, stagger on towards the light,
be loyal, leave behind the louche romances,
scale down the height of all my shoes,
lash my weary person to the mast,
and aim for heaven. *This is how you last,*
they tell me, *cut the sparking fuse;*
a woman doesn't get too many chances.
I wonder if respectable means right;
I'm waiting to be rescued by my doubt.

Toshio Ushiroguchi-Pigott

M.F.M.: Media Friend Marshall

Je me souviens et la Belle Province
McLuhan gives a lecture worried about Separatism
Kanada and "electronic media"
...*wavelengths prior*...
Thank you Marshall.
Oh, and by the way, I read T. S. Eliot's poem
"The Waste Land" and I thought of
Orwellian Absolutism.

"Invisible media"
Social media
Facebook embedding codes proving
your most famous aphorism.

Lazy poetree
Poetree that is struktur'd
Structured media.

Was Chomsky at the G20?
Lippmann I haven't read.
Chomsky I partly read
"Thought control" media
HTML media
Binary-coded media
Media massage therapy
Therapists in the media.

Don't watch T.V.
Big Brother is list'ning too
Can the blind speak?
"Gutenberg" writes and Mae Brown laughs.

Andrea Thompson

I Wouldn't Have Seen It If I Hadn't Believed It: A Probe Poem

It started with Aristotle
and his awkward assertion of Empiricism
all knowledge of the world is procured
from our sensory perceptual system.

Back then we were sure.

Audioception. Gustaoception. Olfacoception.
Tactioception. Ophthalmoception.

We built machines of imitation
attempting to fathom the universe
with our perceptual extensions.

A sixth? Ridiculous myth.
UFOs, Nessie, ESP, Big Foot.

Five.
That's it.
Forever and ever.
Hallelujah.
The end.

Until four more
refused to be ignored
and we reluctantly
let them in.

Equilibrioception. Thermoception. Proprioception.
Nociception.

Andrea Thompson

Educated by animals
our equipment evolved.
Bats taught us sonar
dolphins schooled us
on changes in electrical fields
and sparrows gave lessons
on the earth's magnetic system
by navigating migration each year.

Not content to merely invent sensory tentacles
to explore the edges of our perceptual potential
we went one step further – back to the source
creating machines that mimic how our minds work.

Post-modern, post-industrial
this revolution isn't like the last one
this time we've created an artificial mind
that's changing the way we process information.

It's the *Transformation Theory of Communication* –
in action
McLuhan's *Global Village* – now manifest
we are punch-drunk on civilization
stumbling in a *Narcissus Narcosis* stupor
of chronic overstimulation.

We are disordered, staccato attention spans
meditative canyons – now cracks in the concrete
we are manic, non sequitur, puddle-jumping
surface-surfers
addicted to our oversaturated information receptors.

So I wonder
if the acceleration of our cognitive faculties
will lead to other human perceptual systems
suffering extinction from evolutionary atrophy.

Andrea Thompson

I wonder what will happen
to the wisdom of the belly
our second brain, oft forgotten
though it whispers to us in a language
of a hundred million neurons.

More receptive than a spinal cord
our solar plexus tells us
how we feel about the world
sending butterflies to the cerebral cortex
our gut tells us who to trust
warns us not to get on that bus
and before the phone begins to ring
it lets us know who's calling.

Precognition was once considered
giggle-factor fodder
hocus-pocus
but now that we've proved it
with the Scientific Method
we don't know what to do with it
so we sweep it under the rug
pretend it doesn't exist.

But the confessions of the body
whisper through our nervous system
challenging the gospel of measurable phenomenon
inconvenient truth argues with preexisting hypotheses
as butterflies denounce the mighty God of Certainty.

Even the fabric of the universe
has become conspiring confounder
the cosmos bewilders us
held together by the imperceptible
enigma of dark matter.

Andrea Thompson

Perhaps the lingering dust
of Aristotelian empiricism
is the only variable out of control
making some Scientific Investigation
a megalomania method of conjecture
where hell hath no fury like a theory scorned.

Are ideas life-rafts or a waves in the ocean?
Is knowledge a journey or a destination?

In the two hundred thousand odd years
humans have populated the earth
we've got it wrong – so often
that humble should be our pie du jour.

Post-modern, post-industrial
technology has reached a crescendo of white noise
while the higher wisdom of human intuition
creativity, insight and compassion
still rumbles in our bellies –
a primordial hunger
only humans can fill.

When this revolution reaches its conclusion
an evolution of our perception of wisdom
will become the next terrestrial expedition
will become the mission within that fuels us
that fuses our collective consciousness
from within.

Or maybe not.
How would I know?
I'm just a poet.

An early warning system.
A canary in a coalmine.
A message's medium –

Art Car, Dean Motter

Dale Winslow

Dear Mr. Mössbauer, are you online?

human zenancholy
broken over the photon-
cold lineage of relativity birds
discomforted in the knowledge
that the world will decay.

in another bard-born wakefulness
the sun is no longer needed.

flighting, auger lines
kiss gamma ray marigolds
left solitary as travelers
in universal respiration.

there is no body now.

we are unlinked
pixelated
eternally binary.

dear Sir, trace me.

Dale Winslow

Silent Resonance

Early spring –

the water is cold.
You place your hands
upon it, palms open,
flat, as if to float
upon the surface of life.

This sea –
your life, my life...

all the space between,
invisible, an infinite
expansion,

breathtaking catastrophe.

Along the shore,
you commune, half-despairing
the flesh that holds you in,
wanting to step
out of demanding skin...

To what then?
What is there but this?

Know this is you.

Dimensionless, your fingers
trace the places where life
walks, salvage
the scarred answers,

Dale Winslow

speak the syllables which
existed before sound,

the truth between breaths.

Palms wet,
I hold each side
of your face, beg you to
dissolve,

there is no between...
only here, only this,

your inhale, my exhale

We hunger for effortless language,
stumble over nouns and verbs
that define nothing.

This pantomime repeats,
our invention, our excuse,
a closing act where most fall
gluttonous on indolent pitches,

empty promises of accidental touch.

Elsewhere,
beyond definition
we wheel as one.

I touch
my palms to
water, leaving
your fingerprints.

Dale Winslow

It Was Never a Flower to Begin With

Over the theft of my name,
an incoming desire allies
with a bloody numeral.

My name breaks into realistic sand
and emerges outside the hourglass.
The vowels, the consonants
carry pitfall storms into my house.

Hating my name becomes
an investigative scenario
and your optimistic disclaimer
smacks of copyright.

Outside this deceptive sketch,
your extravagant allotment
is second-hand goods.

Si Philbrook

facebook

step back
step back and see
step back and see it
for what it is...

dot, dot, dot...
advertising bot sucks up your life info,
your online lies; and tries to sell them back to you,
boo hoo,

it is a game,
it baffles me that you can't see it, it wearies me;
"you say it wearies you; But how I caught it, found it,
or came by it,
What stuff 'tis made of, whereof it is born,
I am to learn;"

it is a game, "The medium is the message"
a swimmer without water,
is just a man waving his arms stupidly,
that is us when we do not see
when we do not grasp the simple task at hand,
play it for the game it is

or be like stevie
drowning, not waving.

John Watts

mY parts

"Do you appreciate my parts?"

The waitress turned a shade of numb.

"If only you could see my heart."

She screwed her hair up in a bun.

"You only see my flaccid whole."
"You don't appreciate my soul."
"Some parts of me are beautiful!"

The waitress was struck dumb.

Prose

The invention of prose rendered poetry obsolescent. Poetry can best be understood as the *absence of the prosaic*.

In the absence of the prosaic, we can clearly perceive that we live in an enchanted world. Poetry is the chant, the spell, the glamour that transforms the world, that makes magic from the mundane. In the presence of the poetic, we can discern the spiritual and divine dimensions of creation.

Poetry is sacred, prose is profane. A poetic curse is an affliction. A prosaic curse is profanity.

Poetry elevates discourse. Prose forces language to the ground, making it *prostrate*.

The opposite of prose is amateurs, and the word *amateur* means *lover*. The creation of prose is said to be the world's oldest profession. The creation of prose is called *prostitution*. The composition of poetry is lovemaking. Poetry is love made manifest, love given substance and form.

Poetry finds its home in the human heart. Poetry is therefore easy to learn by heart, while prose is easily forgotten.

Poetry lives in the heart of all humanity as our common inheritance. Everyone is born a poet, singing our first song at the moment of birth, moving on to the pure poetry of infantile babbling and baby talk, and entering a singsong world of nursery rhymes and lullabies. As we grow older, we are weaned away from poetry and force-fed the solid food of prose.

Before prose can take command, poetry must be cut off. We do not give up on poetry all that easily, so it must be surgically removed. Once poetry is amputated, prose can takes its place as a *prosthetic*.

Prose must wage war on poetry, invade and attack poetry, in order to take control over its territory. Prose is the adversary of poetry, seeking to capture, contain, and incarcerate poetry in an offensive that is called *prosecution*.

Prose has its zealots who, with religious conviction, mount a campaign for conversion from poetry by word and by sword. This process is called *proselytizing*.

Before the invention of prose, we had no choice but to remain poetic. Poetry was as ubiquitous, as invisible, as inevitable, and as essential as the air we breathe. We did not even understand or recognize poetry itself, because there was nothing to compare it to. Poetry was all there was.

Before the invention of prose, poetry was our invisible environment. We lived *in* poetry. We worked and played *in* poetry. We ate and drank *in* poetry. We fought and fucked *in* poetry. We prayed and entertained *in* poetry. We spoke, sang, danced, drew, and decorated *in* poetry. We thought, dreamed, and remembered *in* poetry.

Poetry is the first speech of our species, our primal tongue. Prose is our second language, a poor translation of the original utterance.

Poetry is the language of languages, or *metalanguage*.

Poetry is the form of forms, or *metamorphosis*.

Poetry is the secret grammar of grammars that binds the word to the world.

Poetry reveals hidden depths, prose is the slick surface of the mirror, reflecting back only our own image.

Long before the invention of prose, poetry was our most intimate of technologies, the first of the tools and techniques we used to modify our interior landscape. Poetry is the flint we used to cut, scrape, and sharpen our words. Poetry is the fire we used to bring light and heat to the cold darkness of the mind, and also to make raw ideas palatable, transforming them so that they are fit for human consumption, and allowing us to cook up plans and procedures. Poetry is the pottery, baskets, and skins we used to contain our thoughts and our memories.

Long before the invention of prose, poetry was the medium that brought us together as families, clans, tribes, and villages, that connected us and kept us together, preserving and sustaining our ways of life for untold millennia. Poetry was the medium, the container and environment of human culture.

Long before the invention of prose, poetry was the medium of collective memory and collective mind. Poetry predates human consciousness and self-awareness, inner thought and reflection. Poetry gave us something to think with, gave us tools for thought.

The invention of prose rendered poetry obsolescent, freeing poetry to become an art form, and therefore irrelevant.

The invention of prose appeared to be a fatal blow to poetry. The corpse was covered, out of respect, and buried between the covers of the book.

Despite declarations of the innocence of prose in the death of poetry, accusations abounded, many suspecting the presence of a massive conspiracy and cover-up. Rumors spread that poetry was not dead, but living incognito at institutions of higher learning, possibly comatose or suffering from amnesia. Some claim to have spotted poetry in bars and coffee shops, or on street corners.

Few recognized the return of poetry in the form of advertising slogans and jingles, popular songs heard on the radio and recordings, theme music for TV programs, and within online communities of bloggers. The revival of poetry was made possible by the advent of the electronic media environment, which retrieved tribal wisdom and village life on a global scale.

The retrieval of poetry by the electronic media renders prose obsolescent. The recovery of poetry is, in fact, the recovery of humanity, following an extended period of convalescence.

Centenary

Give me that old time commercial Macguffin
I need direction, Spitchcock
Eels wail that, and swell
I am ready for my clothes up
Mr. DeMille shall mug loon
Ear ache, air wreck, ere reckoned
And drew a pondering eye
Extending formal innovation to the causeway
Win again's fake
More shell mock glue-on
Count her blasts, wearing us thin
I'm glistening, come and put me on
Permeating, permit me, per my diem
Martial/artful mech/getta clue on
Mock grew on, menippulating messy jests
The pattern that directs
When the time is ripe
The apple will go to seed
The music will play of its own accordion
Play the record backwards, and it all makes sense
Paul was dead, and now he's better
Metaphysician, obscure thyself!

Biographies

Lillian Allen is a Creative Writing Professor at the Ontario College of Art & Design University in Toronto Canada and an award winning and internationally renowned poet. As one of its lead originators and innovators, she has specialized in the writing and performing of *dub poetry*, a form considered to be a literary godmother of rap, hip-hop and spoken word poetry. Allen is responsible for opening up the form to insist and engrave feminist content and sensibilities. Allen is a multi-talented and multi-faceted artist who also publishes in performance and in a variety of media. A selection of her published works in book and CD formats include: *Psychic Unrest, Women Do This Every Day, Nothing But A Hero, Why Me,* and *If You See Truth.* Her recordings (CDs) include: *Anxiety, Freedom & Dance,* Canadian Juno award winning *Conditions Critical* and *Revolutionary Tea Party.* Allen collaborates with Hamilton, Ontario based visual artist and graphic designer Aaron Mitchell on a regular basis.

Michelle Rae Anderson is a content developer and rogue media ecologist based in Portland, Oregon. Her topical expertise includes Nordic pop music, pie-making, and embedding and interpreting messages in media. She has written a couple of books and hopes to flee (someday soon) to the Netherlands to write another one. Marshall McLuhan is her patron saint and favorite superhero.

Mary Ann Allison is an interdisciplinary scholar at Hofstra University who uses media theory, sociology, and complex systems theory to study the ways in which individuals, communities, and institutions are changing. Before joining the faculty at Hofstra to teach Media Studies, she led global emerging technology projects for Citigroup. In addition to scholarly works, Allison has co-authored a murder mystery and has been a New York City artist in residence for poetry.

Marleen Barr is known for her pioneering work in feminist science fiction and teaches English at the City University of New York. She has won the Science Fiction Research Association Pilgrim Award for lifetime achievement in science fiction criticism. Barr is the author of *Alien to Femininity: Speculative Fiction and Feminist Theory, Lost in Space: Probing Feminist Science Fiction and Beyond, Feminist Fabulation: Space/Postmodern Fiction,* and *Genre Fission: A New Discouse Practice for Cultural Studies.* Barr has edited many anthologies and co-edited the science fiction issue of *PMLA.* She is the author of the humorous campus novel *Oy Pioneer!*

David Bateman is an actor, a spoken word poet, and performance artist presently based in Toronto. He has presented his work internationally and across the country over the past twenty years and also teaches drama, literature, and creative writing at a variety of Canadian post-secondary institutions. His fourth collection of poetry, *Designation Youth*, will be published by Frontenac House Press (Calgary) in the fall of 2014.

Arthur Asa Berger is professor emeritus of Broadcast and Electronic Communication Arts at San Francisco State University, where he taught from 1965 to 2003. He is the author of more than 100 papers and has published 70 books on media, popular culture, humor and tourism. His books have been translated into eight languages and Berger has lectured in more than a dozen countries in the course of his career. He spent a year in Italy as a Fulbright scholar in 1963 and has taught at Jinan University in Guangzhou and Tsinghua University in Beijing. Marshall Mcluhan wrote the introduction to Berger's book *The TV-Guided American.*

bill bissett   originalee from lunaria still trying 2 deepr aquaint with erthling wayze love dewing sound poetee konkreet   innr   splicing narrativ   vizual   shaping langwage thanks 2 andrea thompson who commishyund brush up on yr mccluhan 4 th mcluhan festival held in toronto in part at th gladstone hotel n 2 talonbooks who printid a diffrent versyun in hungree throat my most recent novel both complement each othr n latest cd nothing will hurt   with pete dako n **awesum thanks** 2 lance a. strate n 2 adeena karasick 4 putting ths great book 2gethr

Tony Burgess writes fiction and for film. He lives in Stayner, Ontario.

Jerry Harp's books of poems include *Creature* and *Gatherings.* Among his scholarly studies are *Constant Motion: Ongian Hermeneutics and the Shifting Ground of Early Modern Understanding* and *For Us, What Music? The Life and Poetry of Donald Justice.* He teaches at Lewis & Clark College.

Adeena Karasick is a poet, media ecologist, author of seven books of poetry and poetic theory, and Professor of Pop Culture and Media Theory at Fordham University in New York. Writing at the intersection of Conceptualism and neo-Fluxus performatics, her urban, Jewish feminist mashups have been described as "electricity in language" (Nicole Brossard) and noted for its "cross-fertilization of punning and knowing, theatre and theory" (Charles Bernstein) "a twined virtuosity of mind and ear which leaves the reader deliciously lost in Karasick's signature 'syllabic labyrinth'" (Craig Dworkin). Forthcoming is "Disrobing the Probe, Unpacking the Sprachage: Formal Cause or the Cause of Form: Reframing McLuhan and the Kabbalah" in *Taking Up McLuhan's Cause: Essence and Emergence.*

William Marshe was born in 1966 on Cape Breton Island, Nova Scotia, where he grew up surrounded by art and beauty. He now lives in Toronto, Ontario, where he works as a designer and writes poetry when time, memory and longing allow.

John G. McDaid is a media ecologist and science fiction writer from Brooklyn, New York. He attended the Clarion Science Fiction Workshop in 1993, and sold his first short story, the Sturgeon Award-winning "Jigoku no mokushiroku" to *Asimov's* in 1995. Recently, his "Umbrella Men" was the cover story of the January, 2012 *Magazine of Fantasy & Science Fiction.* A webmaster by day, he lives in Rhode Island and blogs at <http://harddeadlines.com>.

Jill McGinn is an occasionally wizened old bat, born in Cabbagetown, Toronto (specifically St. Michael's Hospital), who has been writing but not publishing since about the age of seven, having never been able to convince herself that it mattered to the progression of her writing or anyone else, such as it is. She has been blessed with a daughter and granddaughter, and while making no firm statements regarding matriarchy, believes that they do impact her ancestry and future. She is the responsible human to a lovely little pitbull named Emma, rescued from the Toronto Humane Society after they were banned on August 29, 2005. Sometimes life gives these gifts, her introduction to bill bissett has been one of those, to be sure. How often, after all, does one meet a lunarian of such epically sweet proportions?

Elizabeth McLuhan is an Independent Writer/Art Curator, based in Nanaimo, BC. Recently, McLuhan guest curated *Vision Circle: The Art of Roy Thomas. A Retrospective Exhibition*, for the Thunder Bay Art Gallery with English/French/Ojibwa catalogue, which continues on national tour through 2014. Throughout her career, McLuhan has combined a passion for history, culture and social justice issues. She has wide experience in both the arts and heritage fields and has been a pioneer in aboriginal art and community based exhibitions at a wide range of museums such as the Art Gallery of Ontario, Canadian Museum of Civilzation and the Royal Ontario Museum. Her shows have traveled nationally and internationally, including an exchange with China. Born in Toronto, McLuhan earned her BA in Fine Arts from Fordham University, New York City, and later pursued an MA in Native/Inuit Art History from the University of New Mexico (Albuquerque). Later she completed her MA/PhD in Medieval Studies from the University of Toronto. She has taught art and history at the University of Winnipeg, Western Michigan University, and the University of Toronto with numerous related publications. Author of *Routes/Roots*, (Toronto, 1974), McLuhan continues to write poetry.

Peter C. Montgomery crept out of Edmonton, AB, Canada to St. Michael's College, the University of Toronto, ON, Canada, where he had classes with Herbert Marshall McLuhan for two wonderful years, as well as some very serious mentoring. McLuhan put Montgomery on to his friends, Sheila and Wilfred Watson for his graduate work, all of which inspired and sustained him in his teaching career in Victoria, BC, Canada.

Dean Motter is a graphic novelist and designer. He studied media and creative electronics under Eric Mcluhan and Tom Lodge at Fanshawe College in London, Ontario in the 70s. He went on with informal post-graduate studies with Eric and his father at the Centre for Culture and Technology, There he was often considered the resident comics artist and authority. Dean is best known for his seminal creation *Mister X,* now published by Dark Horse Comics. He has written *Wolverine* for Marvel, *Superman, The Spirit,* the award-winning 'film-noir' graphic novel, *Batman: Nine Lives* and the acclaimed *Terminal City* series for DC Comics. He is also known for his graphic novel *The Prisoner: Shattered Visage,* based on the 60's British TV series. In his 30+ year-long career Motter has served as art director at CBS Records Canada, DC Comics and Byron Press Visual Publications designing a number of award-winning album covers, graphic novels and book jackets. Further information can be gleaned from <deanmotter.com>.

Alexandra Oliver was born in Vancouver, Canada and divides her time between Toronto and Glasgow, Scotland. The author of two books of poetry, *Where The English Housewife Shines* (Tin Press London) and *Meeting the Tormentors in Safeway* (Biblioasis), she currently teaches in the Stonecoast MFA Program at the University of Southern Maine.

John Oughton is the author of five poetry books, most recently *Time Slip* (Guernica Editions) and somewhere north of 400 articles, reviews, interviews and blogs. He studied writing and literature at York University and the Jack Kerouac School of Disembodied Poetics (Naropa Institute), and is currently Professor of Learning and Teaching at Centennial College in Toronto.

Si Philbrook has been writing poetry for more than thirty years. For twenty of those years his day job was working with and for people with learning disabilities. He lives in Brighton, UK, has two wonderful children, and a large collection of poetry books.

B.W. Powe is a poet, novelist, essayist and philosopher. He teaches Visionary Literature and Media Studies and Creative Writing at York University in Toronto, Canada. He has two books about to be published: *Marshall McLuhan and Northrop Frye, Apocalypse and Alchemy* (University of Toronto Press); and *Where Seas and Fables Meet* (Guernica). He is also at present at work on a g-book ('g' for generative) collaborative process with IN3, the Digital Culture Lab of the Universitat oberta de Catalunya in Barcelona, Spain; it is called *Opening Time: on the Energy Threshold*. "Technogenie" and "Reader" are from a new book of poems called *Invisible Streams*. His last book of poetry, *The Unsaid Passing*, was shortlisted for the ReLit Prize in Canada. His work has been featured in *The New York Times*, *The Globe and Mail*, *The Toronto Star*, and CBC-TV.

Robert Priest is a poet, singer/songwriter, children's author and journalist. His latest books are *Previously Feared Darkness* and the children's book *Rosa Rose* (Wolsak & Wynn). Learn more about Priest at <poempainter.com> and view his performance videos at <youtube.com/greatbigfaced>.

Stephen Roxborough is an author, editor, photographer and graduate of the University of Wisconsin, Madison where he studied English, Art History and McLuhan in the prestigious two-year Integrated Liberal Studies program. UW Madison is also where Marshall McLuhan landed his first teaching job.

Lance Strate is Professor of Communication and Media Studies at Fordham University, a founder and past president of the Media Ecology Association, and a past president of the New York State Communication Association. He is the author of over 100 scholarly articles and several books, including *Echoes and Reflections*, *On the Binding Biases of Time*, and *Amazing Ourselves to Death*. He has also been editor of several journals, including *Explorations in Media Ecology* (which he founded), and co-edited several anthologies, including *The Legacy of McLuhan*. His poems have been published in *Poetica Magazine*, *KronoScope*, *Anekaant*, *ETC*, *Explorations in Media Ecology*, the *General Semantics Bulletin*, and several anthologies. Translations of his writing have appeared in French, Spanish, Italian, Portuguese, Hungarian, Hebrew, Chinese, and Quenya.

Steve Szewczok stems from the island of Cape Breton, Nova Scotia on the east coast of Canada. With a background in theatre and music, Steve has performed in over 50 theatrical productions as well as working in radio and film and writing for the theatre. Steve currently lives in Montreal with his two children and works on the production side of the film industry. *Sugar*, his debut book of poetry, was published in 2012.

Andrea Thompson has performed her poetry at venues across North America and overseas for the past twenty years. She is the co-editor of the anthology *Other Tongues: Mixed Race Women Speak Out*, the author of the poetry collection *Eating the Seed*, and creator of the Urban Music Award nominated CD, *One*. Andrea is a recent graduate of the University of Guelph's MFA Creative Writing program, and currently teaches Spoken Word through the Ontario College of Art and Design's Continuing Studies department. Her first novel, *Over Our Heads*, is due out in the fall of 2014 from Inanna Publications.

Toshio Ushiroguchi-Pigott is a poet and member of Workman Arts, a Toronto based organization which provides individuals with mental illness and addictions issues an opportunity to be creative and have their work showcased. Keeping a journal of his daily life as a mental patient, Ushiroguchi-Pigott is dedicated to exploring poetic themes through the lens of a Mad Poet.

John Watts has recorded 20 albums over the course of a 34-year career, and participated in approximately 3000 concerts and festivals worldwide. He and his band Fischer-Z were signed by UA Records alongside The Buzzcocks and the The Stranglers, and the band toured Europe and North America with artists such as Bob

Marley, The Police and Dire Straits. His first three solo albums included the experimental *The Iceberg Model* (1983). During this period Watts performed to 167,000 people at a Peace Festival in East Berlin alongside James Brown. He made *Destination Paradise* (1991) at Peter Gabriel's Real World studios and his next 3 albums continued to highlight some of the darker areas of human exploitation in their lyrics. He returned solo again with *Thirteen Stories High* (1997) before producing *Bigbeatpoetry* (1999) with DJ Ingo Worner, revealing a radical approach combining poetry, prose and song lyrics. His current era of multimedia solo material began with *Ether Music & Film* (2002), where he travelled internationally in search of random musicians and recorded them in situ on his laptop. *Real Life Is Good Enough* (2004), included a book of poetry and short stories. His last solo release in 2010 *Morethanmusic* added improvised orchestral cut-ups and a filmic dimension. He is the author of a new book of poetry, *The Grand National Lobotomy*, published in conjunction with his World-Go-Round concert, theater, and poetry reading tour.

Dale Winslow is editor-in-chief and publisher at Neo-Poiesis Press. She earned her B.Sc. in Wildlife Management from the University of Guelph and her B.Ed. from the University of Victoria. Dale has been an interpretive naturalist, wildlife and fisheries biologist, teacher, photographer, painter, editor and writer. She was co-editor of the *Poetry Ring* feature for *ETC: A Review of General Semantics* from 2008-2011. Her poetry has been published in *Other Voices, ETC, General Semantics Bulletin*, several anthologies, various e-zines, and she was co-editor and contributor to the poetry anthology *Candy*. She is the author of the full length poetry collection entitled *Tinderbox* (2013).

Dale resides in Victoria on Vancouver Island, British Columbia, Canada.

Tom Wolfe is an American author and journalist best known for his association with New Journalism. A friend and early proponent of Marshall McLuhan, he is the author of 12 nonfiction books, including *The Pump House Gang, The Electric Kool-Aid Acid Test, Radical Chic & Mau-Mauing the Flak Catchers, The Painted Word, From Bauhaus to Our House, The Right Stuff,* and *Hooking Up*, and 4 novels, *The Bonfire of the Vanities, A Man in Full, I Am Charlotte Simmons*, and *Back to Blood.*

Acknowledgments

"The Medium Is..." by Lance Strate originated as the text of a pecha kucha PowerPoint presented at the Media at the Center Marshall McLuhan Centenary Symposium, September 17, 2011, at Fordham University, New York, NY, the 69th Annual New York State Communication Association Conference, October 21-23, 2011, in Ellenville, NY, and the 14th Annual Convention of the Media Ecology Association, at Grand Valley State University, Grand Rapids, Michigan, June 20-23. A video version was uploaded to YouTube on October 31, 2011, and posted on Lance Strate's Blog Time Passing on November 4, 2011.

"Man Made Whole Again" and "Ping-Pong" from "What If He Is Right?" from *The Pump House Gang* by Tom Wolfe. Copyright © 1968, renewed 1996 by Tom Wolfe. Reprinted by permission of Farrar, Straus and Giroux, LLC.

"All the Information in the Sun," Short Sound Poem," and "Micro-Poems" by Robert Priest, from *Previously Feared Darkness* (ECW Press, 2013).

"brush up on yr mcluhan" by bill bissett appeared in a somewhat different version in his novel *hungree throat* (Talonbooks, 2013).

"Self Reflection," "To Sit," "It Came One Day," and "Chop Gently" by Elizabeth McLuhan from *Routes/Roots* (Griffin House, 1974).

"Flash in the Pan" by John McDaid originated as lyrics for the song of the same name on *Media Ecology Unplugged* by Bill Bly and John McDaid <http://www.infomonger.com/meunplug>.

"In My Blogal Village, Print Is Hot" by Adeena Karasick was originally presented at the McLuhan Then Now Next Centenary Conference and DEW Line Festival, Toronto, Ontario, November 7-10, 2011, and at the 13th Annual Convention of the Media Ecology Association, Manhattan College, Bronx, NY, June 2012. A previous version was published on the Marshall McLuhan Galaxy blog, June 12, 2012.

"McLuhan's Bride" by David Bateman from *'tis pity* (Frontenac House, 2012).

"Curriculum Vitae" by Alexandra Oliver from *Meeting the Tormentors in Safeway* (Biblioasis, 2013)

"Silent Resonance" by Dale Winslow from *Tinderbox* (NeoPoiesis Press, 2013).

NeoPoiesis: *a new way of making*

1) in ancient Greece, poiesis referred to the process of making: creation - production - organization - formation - causation

2) a process that can be physical and spiritual, biological and intellectual, artistic and technological, material and teleological, efficient and formal

3) a means of modifying the environment and a method of organizing the self, the making of art and music and poetry, the fashioning of memory and history and philosophy, the construction of perception and expression and reality

4) an independent publisher with a steadfast goal to print and promote outstanding poets, writers and artists that reflect the creative drive and spirit of the new electronic landscape

NeoPoiesisPress.com

www.ingramcontent.com/pod-product-compliance
Lightning Source LLC
Chambersburg PA
CBHW031136090426
42738CB00008B/1113

"If non-believers could learn about Christianity from this book, there would be a lot more believers in the world."

—Tom Nagle, United Methodist pastor (retired), El Paso, Texas

"If you think a book on Christian evidences written by a PhD mathematician must be dry and soulless, think again. Granville Sewell does marshal his sharp intellect in making a case for a cosmic designer of life and the universe, but he writes in a style that is both lively and personable. And when he turns to the case for the God of Christianity, and for Jesus as the crucified and resurrected son of God, Sewell's voice is more than personable; it is heartfelt and at times deeply personal.

"While I differ with Sewell on some of the ways he understands God and Scripture, I am persuaded that this book will prove salutary to many a reader who has always held Christianity at arm's length under the impression that there was only one way that thoughtful and committed Christians can understand God's just nature and his relationship to sinners and suffering in the world. *Christianity for Doubters* accomplishes many things, but if it did nothing more than awaken doubters to some of the variety of thought among faithful Christians on the subjects of suffering and salvation, it would be worth the price of admission. As Sewell shows, Christianity has its beginning and end in the beautiful, courageous, giving, and forgiving person of Jesus Christ, God incarnate. If one allows oneself to meet and fall in love with this most compelling of historical figures, remaining questions can be sorted out with patience and humility."

—Jonathan Witt, Senior Fellow, Discovery Institute's Center for Science and Culture and co-author of *A Meaningful World: How the Arts and Sciences Reveal the Genius of Nature*

"Granville Sewell has written a very well informed and personal book about his Christian faith. He makes a strong and pedagogical case for Intelligent Design, gives a wonderful portrait of Jesus, and has a very honest and touching input to the problem of evil. Although I differ from Granville in some details (I believe in the inerrancy of the Bible, that the world is young, that Adam and Eve were real and that God initially created a world without suffering and death), I still highly recommend *Christianity for Doubters*. This is no doubt a book that many doubters will embrace. It is my prayer that many who read it will accept Jesus into their lives and become Christians."

—OLA HÖSSJER, Professor of Mathematical Statistics,
Stockholm University

"In *Christianity for Doubters*, Granville Sewell makes it clear that Darwin's explanation for evolution requires that the most implausible and improbable developments could happen purely by chance. He makes a compelling case that Intelligent Design is a far simpler explanation for the development of life. He then proceeds to some of the thorniest theological problems that many people have with the Bible and Christianity and addresses them in a clear and straightforward manner."

—H.E. DUNSMORE, Computer Science Professor,
Purdue University

"The overwhelming majority of high school students who attend church stop going once they enter college. A major reason is the lack of training in apologetics—clear, reasoned defenses of their faith. Sewell's book addresses this gap by educating these students and doubters alike about compelling evidence that powerfully affirms the lordship of Jesus Christ."

—ROBERT MARKS II, Distinguished Professor of Electrical
and Computer Engineering, Baylor University

"Senior mathematics professor Granville Sewell has written a fine, short book to give to students going off to college—and others whose environment will test their beliefs. Sewell talks honestly about his faith and his doubts, which gives his testimony considerable value to those who are struggling. His honesty and clarity enable him to make a clear intellectual case for Christianity despite the severe test of a personal tragedy."

—DENYSE O'LEARY, co-author of *The Immortal Mind:
A Neurosurgeon's Case for the Existence of the Soul*